# KEEPING TIME:

Penn Station Clock, New York City

C. Robinson/Courtesy Library of Congress

## *70 Little Stories*

## John Elsing

Elsing, John
*Keeping Time: 70 Little Stories*

ISBN-13: 978-1500862565

Book Layout & Design: Peter O'Toole
Copy Editing: Kathy Ollivier

Printed in the United States of America

# Acknowledgments

I wish to thank several people for their encouragement, forbearance, and help. They are Jonathan Cain, John Cegielski, Joann Cierniak, Herb Coats, Scott Edelstein, Barbara Grudt, Marlyce Helm, Dawn Hetler, Nelly Hewett, Shawn Hollembeak, Kaaren Holum, John H. Hornickel, Scott Lehmann, Tim Maloney, Carol McClellan, Les Metz, Keith Moheban, Kathy Ollivier, Paul Picard, Marlene Reuber, Carol Saunders, Dee Schaefer, Warren Schueneman, R. Andrew Spainhour, and John Toren.

This book is dedicated to Peter O'Toole, Tim Schultz, and Jerry Swenson. Were it not for them, these stories would not be finished.

John Elsing

Minneapolis

2012

# Note to Readers

*Keeping Time: 70 Little Stories* is a collection of true stories. Some names have been changed for privacy's sake.

The stories are arranged chronologically, but each one can stand alone. They are meant to be shared and read aloud as single stories, not as a seamless narrative.

Just as each piece of a patchwork quilt offers a glimpse of something larger, each one of these stories offers a glimpse of the way we were.

*Madam Vigée-Lebrun and Her Daughter Jeanne-Lucie-Louise*, 1789

# Explanation

Next year my ex and I will celebrate fifty years: the first twenty-five together, the last twenty-five apart. Almost half a century has passed since I held Sagi* – not her real name – in my arms for the first time. She is a parent now, just as I was a parent then. We are moving through the generations that define us: child, parent, grandparent.

Through it all, our memories – sometimes brightening, other times darkening – have kept us company. From time to time they turned themselves into little stories. I have collected seventy of them here. I wrote them down to help us keep the past from fading away.

Like the students in the well-known Psychology 101 experiment, we do not always remember things happening in the same way, but for the most part, we can still find the path back to moments when the clock stood still, enabling us to see, not just what the camera sees, but what is there.

---

\* The "gi" in Sagi is pronounced like the "gi" in *Gigi*, the 1958 movie that won nine Oscars and made Leslie Caron famous.

"The universe is made of stories, not of atoms."
—Muriel Rukeyser, *The Speed of Darkness (1968)*

# KEEPING TIME: 70 Little Stories

Avenue of Trees

# Keeping Time

Not possessing Proustian gifts,
one forgets,
little by little,
what long-ago times were like.

Today,
as I look back
and try to remember,
I can only catch glimpses of the way we were.

Now and again
a detail
or two
will stand out.

Something takes one's attention for a minute,
but then it,
too,
slips away,
back into the blur.

One makes an effort to get what has gone before to stand still,
the better to observe it,
but it wriggles and jiggles and escapes our grasp,
precluding closer examination.

Occasionally one can recall times when the moving finger
stopped
for a moment,
but when one catches up,
it has moved on,
closer to the edge of oblivion.

Try though we do to capture it,
the past keeps slipping away –
until we find that we can regard a year,
or more,
without so much as a sentence comment.

Although our bodies cannot,
our memories can,
almost magically,
leap over mountains of time
until we find ourselves facing that second vast eternity.

# Memorial Day, 2008

It is six o'clock in the morning here in Minneapolis, Minnesota, the "City of Lakes," where I saw my daughter, Sagi, for the first time more than forty years ago. She was tiny, yet she rested comfortably in the bend of the nurse's arm and seemed to regard her surroundings with keen interest. Her gaze was steady, reserved, and alert. She held her right hand out in front of her as if waiting for someone to take hold of it.

Chrislofoto/Shutterstock.com

Military Cemetery

# Saturday's Child

I followed the nurse down the hall as she carried Sagi in her arms. No one else was around. When we reached the nursery, I opened the door, closed it after them, and stepped over to the window to look inside. The nurse walked to an incubator on the far side of the room and gently lowered Sagi into it. Only a few other babies in bassinets were in the place. They were not close to the window the way they are in *The New Yorker* magazine cartoons. I stood there for a long time, alone, just watching. After a while the nurse left. I stayed, thinking I could always run in to save the children in case there was a fire or an explosion – then I wondered where such thoughts come from.

It was Saturday morning. I could stay as long as I wanted. At some point someone brought me a chair. "Saturday's child works hard for its living" passed through my mind. I thought of my friend Polly. When we were first introduced, she had referred to herself as a Cape Cod girl, even though she was Boston-born and bred, not a Cabot or a Lodge, but close. Polly told me that once, when she was little, she had asked her father if they were rich; he had answered,

"Richer than many, poorer than some." He went on to say, "It's best to work for one's living, as I do," adding that he thought working had kept him halfway normal, had maybe even saved his sanity. Polly was grateful to him for these words. After his death she learned he had followed his own advice; he never touched the money his parents had left in trust for him.

# Only to God

When I woke up later that morning, stretched out on a sofa in a private waiting room, it was already eleven o'clock. At first I didn't know where I was and couldn't remember how I had come to be there. Slowly, I stood up, made my way to the nursery, and took a place at the window. Sagi was lying in her incubator along the far wall, away from the bassinets, most of which were empty. She was moving her arms and legs. "That's a good sign," I thought, but she was red all over, like my own color when I've been in the sun too long. That worried me. Was it too warm in there for her? Might she be harmed if her arms or legs touched the sides of the incubator? Should I call a nurse? On the other side of a window wall, just beyond Sagi, several nurses were talking together, and laughing, maybe even drinking coffee. I couldn't tell for sure. "They should be looking after those babies," I thought, "and not just passing the time of day like that."

They were all deaconesses, dressed in the same plain way, but there seemed to be some kind of hierarchy, possibly something to do with the caps. Whatever it was, one of them looked better turned out, more starched than the others. It wasn't long before this nurse looked up, saw me, and motioned to indicate that she was coming out. Relieved, I moved to open the door for her. She thanked me, greeted me by name, and said she was in charge of the nursery unit; did I have any questions? I mentioned the temperature in the incubator. She assured me it was fine and asked if I had already had a chance to hold Sagi in my arms. When my eyes filled with tears, she said, "Would you like to hold her now?" "Yes," I replied, "if you have the time, and if it wouldn't be too much trouble." "No, it won't be any trouble at all," she said. "That's why nurses are here." She pointed in the direction of a small adjoining room and told me to go in and take a seat. She would bring Sagi to me. Then she turned and went back into the nursery.

I watched as she opened the incubator and carefully lifted Sagi out, wrapping her in a light blanket as she did so. She brought Sagi to me, settled herself in a big chair, and I sat down in the chair next to it. Sagi was asleep. She was beautiful. The nurse positioned Sagi on my left arm and placed my right hand gently against Sagi's back, to serve as support. I was afraid Sagi would awaken, but she didn't. There I was. I had never held a baby before, and this child was the first person I had ever seen who shared my blood.

# Whence

May, 2008

I was born in 1938, seventy years ago this month, the Biblical threescore years and ten, in Minneapolis General Hospital, now called Hennepin County Medical Center. Sagi was born in 1966 at Lutheran Deaconess Hospital, a little more than a mile away. HCMC is still there. Lutheran Deaconess is not. When I mustered the courage and returned to the Deaconess site a few days ago, for the first time in more than forty years, I found a vacant lot.

As I held Sagi in my arms on the first day of her life, I tried to imagine what things were like when I was born. Someone must have held me, too, but I don't know who that might have been. Sagi is the first person I have ever seen who is biologically related to me. My mind tries to comprehend what that means, but fails. It is like looking at a bright light – one can't get through to its source, or see what's behind it. I have to look away. My concentration glances from one side of it to the other, sliding about like an electric drill from one part of a steel plate to another. I try to grasp what it means to share a bloodline with someone. I don't succeed. After a while,

I stop trying, but something has changed. No great cloud of peace came and wrapped itself around me, yet I remember feeling grateful. The nurse tells me there is nothing to worry about. "Sagi is small," she says, "but she's strong. She'll be fine."

* * * * * * *

One day seven years later as Sagi and I were walking into town together, she asked, "Daddy, where did I come from?" A moment passed, and then I answered, "Sagi, dear, you just sprang from my loins. There was no holding you back."

She wanted to know what loins are and where to find them. With both my hands I patted myself below the belt and said, "They're in here, Sagi, right here; this is where you came from."

More than a quarter century after that, I asked a friend of mine – a man who had never married – if he had wanted to have children. I saw emotion track across his face and heard it in his voice as he looked at me and said, "Oh, yes, I did, very much." In that moment I remembered what it had been like to hold Sagi for the first time, knowing that no matter what other blessings might come my way, nothing could ever take her place.

# The Second Day

Early the next morning, Sunday, I returned to the hospital and spent the day there. Before going to work on Monday, I stopped by to see how things were going. After work I went to spend the evening with my new family.

Life went on like this for the next few days. Sagi's weight dropped a little, not much, but the doctor said that was to be expected, and she thrived from then on. She was always wide awake in the morning and usually woke up when she was brought to me in the evening. I held her while she had her supper. Sagi usually napped for a while after eating, and then I cradled her in my arms. She turned in early, and so did I.

Years ago I heard a story about an elderly Frenchwoman who was asked if she was happy. She considered the question, and then she said, "Happy? No, I am too old for 'happy,' but maybe one could say I am content."

Sagi was perhaps too young for "happy," but she seemed content. I never saw her cry. She was a good observer. I noticed that she paid attention to what was going on around her. Best of all, the nurse told me that Sagi knew who I was. She seemed comfortable in my arms. I hoped she felt – or was beginning to feel – some kind of connection to me.

A few weeks before Sagi was born, I read an article in *The New York Times Magazine* that said infants always look into the eyes of the person feeding them. The idea appealed to me. Now I had the opportunity to confirm this for myself. It was true. I watched Sagi as she ate and saw her looking back at me. I decided never to let her look up and find me not looking back at her, taking an interest in what she was doing. I wanted her to know that I, too, was paying attention.

# Disillusioned Idealist

My grandmother always gave me her full attention. Maybe she was a bit mystified by the little boy who had been adopted by her son and his wife. She told me things I don't think she shared with her other grandchildren: how she considered it bad form to make, or repeat, jokes about Frisians (she had emigrated from the Netherlands), or Iowans (she had moved there from Chicago), or any other group of people. "Do unto others," she would say, "as you would have others do unto you, and don't forget that the hottest spots in hell are reserved for those who think they are somehow better than other people." She had been taught to look for the best in everyone, and she practiced what she had been taught all her life. I know she looked for the good in me, even when it was hard to find, or, as she might have put it, when the pail came up empty.

One day a neighbor backed his horse trailer into the right-rear fender of Grandma's tan and cream-colored Ford, shattering the red glass housing of the taillight, and doing other damage as well. We all went out to see what had happened, and Grandma tried the lights. They were still in working order, but when I saw the taillight blinking white, I started to cry and behaved badly. I said I thought it was unfair that a white light should try to fool us into thinking it was red when, really, the light wasn't red at all; it was only the glass that was red.

No one else standing out there understood what had upset me so much, but Grandma took the time to listen to me. She figured out that I thought lights came in different colors. She didn't try to explain it. Instead of asking me to go back in the house, she took me aside, patted me on the head and said, "There, there, my little Hamlet, it's all right." That distracted me, and I began to calm down. As soon as I decently could, I asked, "Who is Hamlet?"

# Johann Sebastian Bach, 1685 – 1750

Soon after Fanny Mendelssohn was born, her mother asked to see her. The baby girl was wrapped in warm blankets and taken to her mother's room. After looking at her daughter for a while, Mrs. Mendelssohn asked the nurse to undo the blankets a little so she could see Fanny's arms and hands. This was done. "Oh, good," she said, "Bach fugue fingers. One day they will be perfect for playing Bach." This was in 1805. Fanny's brother, Felix, was born four years later, in 1809. Both children were prodigies. They shared their love of music with each other throughout their lives.

When Fanny began composing, she published her work under her brother's name. In those days accomplishment of that sort was considered unseemly in a woman. Later, Felix regarded this as an error on his part and helped Fanny publish under her own name. As history shows, the Mendelssohns were a remarkable family that expanded to include Fanny's husband, Wilhelm Hensel, who also loved music and encouraged his wife in her work.

Felix Mendelssohn organized a performance of Bach's *St. Matthew Passion* in 1829. It was the first time the work had been heard in concert since Bach's day.

\* \* \* \* \* \* \*

As I held Sagi in my arms, saw the intensity of her gaze, and felt the strength with which she was able to grasp my fingers, I hoped she would want to play Bach on the piano, join in singing his music, and one day appreciate and be sustained by his monumental gift. As she squeezed my hand again and again, I wondered if she was trying to tell me something, maybe, "Daddy, don't let go of me." I hoped she could somehow understand that, as I held her hands and kissed them, I was hoping to say that I would try never to let go of her, that I would always, for as long as I was able, try to be there for her, just like the art of Bach.

*Johann Sebastian Bach.*

# At Home

It was two o'clock in the afternoon. Sagi seemed to be wide awake, but she fell asleep almost immediately after I placed her in her new bed. I knew she would nap for an hour or so and be hungry when she woke up. I went to the kitchen to prepare the formula. It had to be heated and then left to cool before going into the refrigerator.

After dinner that evening there was quiet time together before she fell asleep for the night. I read a few pages of Sigrid Undset's book, *Kristin Lavransdatter*, and then did the laundry. It took some getting used to, but Sagi would be a baby only once. This wasn't going to happen to me again. It was the last time I would be traveling this road.

Sometimes she slept in my arms. Other times I fell asleep at the side of her bed; when I woke up, her hand would still be resting on mine. In the days that followed, Sagi established her own routine, and I accustomed myself to it. I napped when she napped. In the evening I usually went to bed soon after she did. The time passed quickly.

With a baby to care for, life was reduced to basic matters:

eating, sleeping, keeping things clean, and holding her. I enjoyed it. I gave myself over to family life. The nurses told me I would not have to worry about finding time to get things done, that babies are like pets, they sleep a good part of the day. "You will have plenty of time to adjust," they said, and that's what happened. The pediatrician said I would "grow into it," and I did. "Before you know it," he said, "you will become so accustomed to having a baby in the house you'll wonder how you ever managed to live without her." He was right about that, too.

Egg Chair

# Egg Chair

It was during a visit to Copenhagen, Denmark, that I saw an egg chair for the first time. There were several of them together in a display window. They looked a little like abstract representations of some large, long-extinct bird that Henry Moore might have used for inspiration at his studio in England. They were, in fact, from the workshop of Arne Jacobsen, a Danish architect who designed them in 1958 for the SAS Royal Hotel in Copenhagen. The egg chair is a modern interpretation of the traditional wing chair. I thought it was the most handsome chair I had ever seen.

A few years later I saw them again. This time they were in a magazine in a Chicago library. They were pictured in the Manhattan apartment of Mr. and Mrs. Richard Rodgers. "Large chairs don't get any better than this," I said to myself. In the fifty years since they were introduced, I don't think they have ever been surpassed. Now they are almost too famous; one sees them on television, in the movies, as well as in magazines. Egg chairs are special: they are to chairs what the Eiffel is to towers.

More years passed, and then, early one November morning, I

looked out the front windows and saw a van with the name "Airborne" lettered on its side. It was stopping at our house. Our first egg chair had arrived from the Fritz Hansen factory in Denmark.

It was there, ready and waiting, when Sagi came home from the hospital a few months later. It was in that chair that she had her meals. It was where we sat together when I sang to her and read her stories. While in this chair, she slept in my arms – curled up between my elbow and the curved tips of my fingers – and it was here that I would look into her eyes and always find her looking back at me.

Until Sagi left for college, this chair, joined later by two others just like it, shared our space. Every morning when we came down the stairs, there they were, waiting, as if to welcome us back to a conversation they had carried on without us all through the night.

The chairs turned so easily they often rotated a little in the night air, to the right or the left, and ended up facing in different directions; sometimes they turned around completely, so the three of them presented us with a new configuration in the morning. Some days we found them looking out the windows; other times they turned their backs on one another, but every morning it was something new. I think they did it to amuse us.

# One Hand Clapping

At the beginning of his book, *The Growth of Love*, John Bowlby, the English psychologist, says that a child whose mother figure is interrupted during the first two years of its life suffers an injury to its abstract reasoning powers. Reading that, I realized that what he was saying applied to me. I was adopted when I was eight months old. I wondered if Sagi would also encounter problems with things like math, chemistry, physics, music theory, philosophy, pinochle, tying knots, and chess.

As the years passed, I asked several psychologists about this. Even though most were acquainted with Dr. Bowlby's work, and all knew him by reputation, none of them remembered what he had said about abstract reasoning and mothering. Their reactions to what I was saying ranged from polite, "That's an interesting idea," to the startled, "My God, if that is true, the implications for many adopted children are huge."

When I mentioned Dr. Bowlby's work to Dr. Dale Jorgenson at Fairview Southdale Hospital in Edina, Minnesota, he, too, listened, maybe a bit skeptically at first, but when I told him that I had done reasonably well in school until I had to take algebra as a ninth-grader, he interrupted and said, "That makes sense to me because, when I was a boy, my best friend, like you, was adopted. The two of us were quite evenly matched in most everything we did, that is, until we started algebra. At that point he began to fall behind, and what he told me then is the same thing you are telling me now – that despite his best efforts, he could not understand it."

Abstract reasoning powers cannot be seen. If they are injured, it's not likely they can be fixed. That's all there was to say about that. We returned to the business at hand. "It's for someone to try to solve at some point in the future," I thought, "and I am stuck in the here and now. I have to try to make the best of it." I remembered the words of Theodore Roosevelt: "Do what you can, where you are, with what you have." And what I had was a child to raise.

# Asleep at the Switch

Today is July 21, 2008. Thirty-nine years ago this morning, I lifted Sagi into her highchair, sat myself down, and we started on breakfast.

"How are you this morning?" I asked.

"I know what happened yesterday," she said.

"You do? That's good," I said. "What happened yesterday?"

"Astronauts walked on the moon," she answered, adding they had worried that the spindly legs of the lunar module might sink into the moon's surface, thus causing the LM to tip. "If it tipped too much," she said, "the astronauts would have to stay on the moon because the lunar module would not be able to return to the spacecraft circling overhead."

"So what did they do to try to prevent that from happening?" I asked.

"They attached a big metal saucer to the bottom of each leg so the lunar module couldn't tip to the side, or fall over."

"That's good, Sagi," I said. "Can you see the pictures of the astronauts and the moon in your head?"

"Yes, I can," she answered.

"Will you try to keep them there until tomorrow morning?" I asked.

"Yes, I will," she said.

She was a month short of being three years old. I was half a year older than that on December 7, 1941, and still remember the day Pearl Harbor was bombed. With a little help, I hoped Sagi would be able to remember the moon landing for a long time.

\* \* \* \* \* \* \*

In December, 1941, my parents and I went to visit relatives in White Bear Lake, north of St. Paul, not far from Dellwood, where F. Scott Fitzgerald and his wife, Zelda, had lived for a time. We took the train from Worthington, the same station my father's younger cousins, George and Ernie, left from when they went away to war a few months later. We were in the Twin Cities to go Christmas shopping at Dayton's in Minneapolis.

In my mind's eye, I can still see the adults sitting around the dining room table in the early afternoon on the Sunday of the attack in Hawaii. They were talking about President Franklin Delano Roosevelt, FDR. They said he had been caught "asleep at the switch." I wondered why the President was out on the railroad tracks next to what I thought was a switch, and how he could have fallen asleep there. I remember there was apple pie for dessert.

The house where we stayed had an orchard, and there was a large, screened room between the house and the garage.

When the pie was all gone, I went outside to play. It was unseasonably warm, and the snow was melting. There were little streams of water flowing down both sides of the street that led to White Bear Lake. Through the trees I could see the lake a block or two away. I found sticks on the lawn and broke them into pieces as long as my arms. They had been lying on the ground for a long time and were easy to break. I placed them, one after the other, in the water and ran after them as they made their way down the street toward the lake. I imagined they were a fleet of ships steaming out to sea. I wished the battleships in Honolulu could do the same, but I knew they couldn't. They had been trapped in the harbor; some of them had been sunk. I understood what that meant. Many sailors had died. It made me sad.

* * * * * * *

Next year it will be forty years since astronauts first walked on the moon. Sagi still remembers the day. Two years after that, it will be seventy years since the attack on Pearl Harbor.

# Eternity

I.　　Life after Death

There are as many ways to think about death as there are people on the planet. They vary from the flip to the philosophical, but one thing is certain: sooner or later, death comes for everyone.

William Shakespeare described our little life as rounded with a sleep. Vladimir Nabokov likened life to a brief ray of light between two vast eternities. Most people who read Jean Paul Sartre's *Being and Nothingness* probably dwell more on the former than on the latter.

Whether we believe the idea of eternal life or eternal death, lawyers know that when it comes to thinking about the hereafter, most people are – to a greater or lesser extent – in a state of denial. We prefer not to think about eternal anything. Because we don't see death every morning at breakfast, or standing on the street corner waiting for a bus in the afternoon, there is a tendency not to think about it at all, or, at the very most, very little.

Out of sight, out of mind. We tend toward the idea that the

living hold the majority, but they are really only the very thin edge of that vast number of those who, because of some cosmic quirk, escaped the void for a time and then had to return to it. Rather than consider the alternative, we prefer to keep on dancing in the lovely light. Anything is better than thinking about how quickly we are using up our allotted number of tomorrows. And maybe it's just as well that way, for the deep thinkers tell us that if we could fathom the meaning of death for even the smallest part of an instant, it would kill us, and why would we want that? If that were to happen, what would have been the use of all our philosophy? No, maybe it's best, during this brief respite from the dark, that we play while the lights are still on, because it is the only chance we're ever going to have to see what's happening out there on the field of life. Soon enough, the power will fail – or the plug will be pulled – and we, too, will be taken out of the game and sent back to the dark of the dugout from which no one returns.

## II.   Don, the Gorilla

The first time I saw Don, the gorilla, I was a young man with children.  Don was still a baby.  Although baby gorillas usually stay with their mothers for three or four years, Don had been separated from his mother when he was younger than that.  The last time I saw Don I was an old man, and Don had been dead for fourteen years.

Because I was not in Cameroon, Africa, when Don was born in 1968, I could not welcome him to life, but I was in St. Paul to remember him when he died of liver failure in 1994 at the age of twenty-six.  The average life span for Western Lowland gorillas is thirty to fifty years, so Don died at a relatively young age, before his time, as they say.  He weighed more than twice as much as I do and was roughly a foot shorter than I am.  Instead of one-of-a-kind paw prints, he had, like all gorillas, a unique nose print.  Red-headed gorillas are common in Cameroon, and Don had some red hair.

Gorillas do not drink water.  They get all the moisture they need from the approximately fifty pounds of foliage they eat every day, but Don doesn't have daily feedings any more.  He resides instead in a climate-controlled, glass-walled enclosure called a taxidermy mount in the Science Museum of Minnesota, where he is a favorite exhibit of the people who visit there, just as he was when alive and living with his countrywoman gorilla, Donna, at the Como Park Zoo in St. Paul.  Tim Bovard, the taxidermist of the Los Angeles County Museum of Natural History, has given Don a lease on a different kind of life after death.

For a long time, when we were all younger, Sagi and I visited Don and Donna in their hall at the zoo every Sunday morning. Don, especially, liked the attention, and we liked him. Sometimes, maybe to remind us they were animals, Don did things that caused onlookers to turn away quickly, but it didn't matter. Such behavior kept a tight rein on sentimentality.

Now we can go to the Science Museum in St. Paul and remember Don as he was back then: affectionate, content, mischievous, patient, playful, and smiling. If we could ask him, and if he could answer, would he say he's a lucky gorilla, to be as popular in death as he was in life? Or would he say, "It's not life, but it's not bad." And wouldn't we have to agree with him? To be remembered for our good qualities and have the bad ones forgotten, surely that is something to hope for. Maybe Don would just smile and say nothing, marveling that, of all the gorillas ever born, he was chosen to be a taxidermalogical triumph.

# The Cream in Your Tea

Some families have Meissen, others have Limoges or Royal Doulton. Our porcelain was from Porsgrund, in Norway.

I went to Norway with the Augustana College Choir in 1960. One day we visited the Porsgrund Porcelain factory. A pattern called "Blue Lines and Flowers on White" captured my attention, and I bought as many pieces as my travelers checks would allow. Today this pattern is no longer in production at Porsgrund. Original pieces are almost impossible to find, but there are many variations available from other sources.

The blue color on our white porcelain is not the color one associates with the British Admiralty, nor is it like the inky blue one sometimes sees in Rosenthal. It isn't as dark a blue as that made by Royal Danish Copenhagen. It is a lighter shade of blue, rather like the color one finds in those blue and white striped shirts from Brooks Brothers that were popular a generation ago and which can still be seen occasionally in places that have long memories, like the Department of State in Washington, D.C. They were worn with regimental ties and gray herringbone jackets, or with navy blue blazers that were part of a look that was once regarded as the very glass of fashion. Times change, however, and one day in the 1990s I heard someone say that people who dressed like that looked like characters who had escaped from the Seattle Light Opera Company.

In the Far East as well as here in the West, however, blue and white in porcelain has never gone out of style. The combination possesses a timeless quality that transcends fashion. Through the years, a great many people – from Japan to Amsterdam – have continued taking their tea from blue and white cups.

The Dutch, it is said, drink more tea per capita than any other nationality in the world, including the English and the Chinese. Many of them make a cup of tea for themselves first thing in the morning. Farmers in Holland have a cup of tea at five a.m. before going out to do the milking. What the English call "elevenses" is just another cup of tea in the Netherlands. There is also afternoon tea and a last cup of tea before going to bed at night.

The Dutch drink tea almost as often as monks pray, and they don't consider it sacrilegious to take cream with it. My grandmother taught me how to hold a teaspoon of cream over the tea, letting the spoon touch the inside of the cup, and then to tip the spoon slowly toward the rim so the cream slides down to the bottom. Droplets of cream will then rise to the surface and silently explode there, making tiny "flowers" that are remarkably remindful of those one sees in the "Blue Lines and Flowers on White" pattern. Most children, like Sagi, and many adults as well, will smile when they see this happen. If they do not, try again another day with different guests.

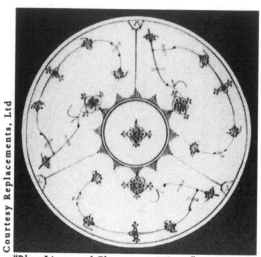

"Blue Lines and Flowers on White," Porsgrund

## Sesame Street

*Sesame Street* appeared on PBS for the first time in November of 1969. The series generated a lot of interest both here and abroad. People had high hopes for it, but it wasn't long before there were reports of children banging things around when the programs were over. Some children seemed to find it difficult to return to self-generated play. Sagi and I watched the first program together. Remembering this forty years later, I don't think either of us knew quite what to say when it ended. Sagi never asked to see it again, and that was fine with me.

The creators of *Sesame Street* deserve high marks for the attention they brought to children, but they made a mistake when they decided to use the commercial TV ad as their model. TV ads do not invite viewers to give their attention; on the contrary, with their heightened action, volume, and quick cuts, they compel attention from those who watch, rather like lightning. Once a taste for lightning excitement has been instilled in viewers, it's not easy for them to appreciate the serenity of a sunset.

Instead of using excitement to cater to the short attention span of children, it might have been better if they had tried to lengthen the ability to pay attention, but that was not to be. Parents soon found that many children didn't like it when the television was turned off. Living without the TV crutch was hard to do. It is a skill that many people, not just children, need help in mastering.

Time passed, and children weaned on talking rabbits started school. When their parents asked them, "How was school today?" an elongated cry of *boring* rang out across the land.

There were some who raised objections to the frenetic pace of television, but it was easy for the powers that be to ignore them. This was not a topic that was going to be welcome on the morning TV talk shows.

Other countries acquired the rights to *Sesame Street*. Some of them cut out the shorter segments, then slowed down and lengthened others. Long concerned about the effects of over-stimulation on the young, some places had rules against taking small children into movie theaters, but that kind of thinking had never been popular in the United States. Powerful forces in this country, lobbying for their own self-interests, said it was up to parents to decide what was best for their children.

"*Titanic* for two-year-olds, what's wrong with that?" they asked, and added, "It's a free country, isn't it?"

The word "hyper" became a basic component of conversation, followed soon by Attention Deficit Disorder. The country's children and those who looked after them were paying a heavy price for a steady stream of TV excitement. Too few people were concerned about the quality of life that awaited children when the television screen went dark.

An old Chinese proverb says it is better to teach people how to feed themselves than to keep feeding them day after day. Many caregivers agree it is better for children to engage in active play than it is for them to be sedentary. A lot of people, over the years, predicted the obesity crisis that now confronts us, but they were not given much of a hearing because it was not in the financial interest of commercial television to have people turn off the TV.

Parents who bought toys from Creative Playthings were dismayed when CBS bought the New Jersey company in the late 1960s. Although the press release assured customers that everything would continue unchanged, few people were naïve enough not to see the handwriting on the wall. Creative Playthings, as we had known it, slowly disappeared.

It wasn't until the 1970s that Norman Cousins, editor of the influential *Saturday Review*, expressed some reservations about *Sesame Street*. Because Mr. Cousins could not be ignored, it became possible for ordinary folk to voice their misgivings about the program. In the years that have passed since then, *Saturday Review* has also disappeared.

Those who compare television broadcast systems in countries around the world, like Dr. Donald R. Browne at the University of Minnesota, have said for a long time that America's commercial television industry would do well to turn the spotlight on itself, but that is not likely to happen anytime soon.

# Mystery House

"I'm going to walk into town; would you like to come along?" I asked. Sagi looked up from what she was doing and said, "Which streets are you taking?"

"I'm taking a new route," I answered, "past something you've never seen before."

"How can you do that?" Sagi asked. "We know every street and alley in St. Anthony Park."

"Oh," I said, "you'll find out. There are still some things waiting to be discovered around here."

"I'm going with you," she said.

I gathered up my wallet, keys, and handkerchief. It was summer. We didn't need jackets. After closing the back gate, I asked if she wanted to try walking with her eyes closed. We had been taking turns doing that for weeks, ever since she read about Helen Keller.

"Yes," she said, "I'll keep my eyes closed on the way to Micawber's Bookstore, and you can keep yours closed on the way back."

"Fine," I said, giving her the blue-and-white bandana that we used as a blindfold. She put it on, spun herself around, asked for the walking stick, and started out.

I helped her across the uneven surface of the field rock driveway. We walked out of the alley and down to Grantham Street where we made a right turn and, a minute or two later, a left. Shortly after that I found myself looking up at one of the first houses built in the University Grove neighborhood. Its owners always said they were told to choose their own house number, so they picked 1564, the year of William Shakespeare's birth. A half block beyond that house, as Sagi and I left Hoyt Avenue for Branston Street, I found what I was looking for.

A family by the name of Donaldson lived in a half-timbered house on this corner. The front door opened onto Hoyt. For that reason there was no sidewalk leading up to the house from Branston. This made for an unbroken expanse of lawn larger than what one usually saw in this part of town. "That's good," I thought. I hoped Sagi would not recognize it. There was a one-story sunroom on the Branston side of the house. That, too, was unusual. It looked out on a garden set with small trees and evergreen shrubs. Maybe it had escaped Sagi's notice as well. When I looked at the sunroom and shut out the rest of the house with my hands, it was surprising to think we were only three blocks away from home. Perfect.

We walked south on Branston until we were in line with the sunroom windows. At that point I asked Sagi to stand still for a minute.

"Keep your eyes closed, but take your blindfold off." She did that.

Then I said, "I am going to cup my hands around your eyes," and I did that. "Now, open your eyes. What do you see?"

"I see a sliver of light," she said.

"What else do you see?" I asked as I moved my hands a little farther apart.

"I can see some windows in a house," she said.

"Good, how many windows?" I asked. "Two," she answered.

I opened up my hands a little more. "Tell me when you can see four."

"I see four," she said.

"Can you see the bushes to the right and left of the windows?" I asked.

"Yes," she said. "Are they like the big arborvitae bush that the Schoberg boy moved from in front of our living room windows to the side of the front lawn?" she asked.

"Yes," I answered. "Take a good look. This is the mystery house. Try to remember it."

Sagi looked at it. When she was finished, I asked her to close her eyes again. Then I took my hands away and put the bandana back in place.

"So," I said, "do you know where you are?"

"No," she said, "you told me you were taking a new route,

that's why."

"You are right," I said.

Sagi and I lived in that neighborhood until she went away to college. Occasionally she asked me where the mystery house was, but I never told her. Instead, I saved it for today. She will learn the answer to that question when she reads this.

# Spelling

I had some problems in school, but spelling was never one of them. I always liked spelling and often wished I could take part in a spelling bee somewhere, but my teacher said that spelling bees were for people who wanted to show off. When Sagi came home with her first spelling test, I saw that she hadn't done very well. I was surprised, and maybe she was, too. "Did you perhaps study the wrong list of words?" I asked. She assured me she had studied the words that were on the test, then added that she wasn't very good at spelling.

"It's probably something we need to work on," I said. "I'm sure your spelling will get better soon."

Sagi didn't seem so certain, but we didn't say anything more about it. A week later she showed me the second spelling test. The results were not as good as those from the first. I asked her if she would like me to help her study for the next test, but she said, "No." As softly as I could, I asked, "Why not?"

"Well," she said, "Oona's mother said not to worry about it because spelling is not a sign of intelligence. She said that even monkeys can learn to spell. It's like driving a car – monkeys can learn to do that, too."

I told her about my college housemate, a man whose name she knew well, and how spelling had always been a tribulation for him. He worked hard to overcome the problem, but never quite succeeded.

Sagi asked, "But you still like him, don't you?"

"Yes," I said, "I do. He's my best friend, and people love their children, too, no matter what their schoolwork is like. You know that, don't you?" I asked.

"Well, that's all right then," she said.

"Yes, it is," I continued, "but just because we are not so good at something does not mean we should stop working at it. It's not always easy, either, for people to remember to say "Please" and "Thank you," but that doesn't mean they need not try to be polite to one another. Besides, it's fun to be able to spell well."

"But there are so many words in the dictionary. How will I ever be able to learn all of them?" she wanted to know.

"Don't worry," I said, "you don't have to learn every word in *Webster's Third*. For now, let's just work on the words you've had trouble with so far. How would that be? Would you like to go to Miller's corner store to buy a special notebook, one just for spelling words that you want to practice? We'll write down the words you misspell in that notebook and then, every night, before you fall asleep, we'll go over those words together and, maybe, if we do that

*44*

for a while, the big word processor in your head will reprogram itself, something like that."

"There are a lot of words I don't know how to spell," she said. "What will we do if we fill all the notebooks they have at Miller's? We'd better start building more bookshelves for all the notebooks we will need."

We bought a loose-leaf ring binder and lots of dividers. Sagi chose them. Grouping the words alphabetically made them easier to find, and we were less likely to enter a word twice.

The next Saturday afternoon Sagi wrote all the words she had misspelled in the new notebook. That same evening, before she fell asleep, I read each word, and she tried to spell it. We placed an X next to those words that gave her the most trouble. I can't say we made a game of it, but it was agreeable work. It became part of our routine, and neither of us minded it too much.

As the months passed, the number of words in the notebook grew, and Sagi learned how to spell many of them correctly. We penciled out words when they became easy for her.

We didn't practice spelling while on vacation, the way some of our neighbors over on Hoyt Avenue did, but when we were at home, even on weekends, we remembered to work at it. Sagi's tests improved. It took time, but the day arrived when  spelling was no longer a problem for her.

# Bockman Hall

In Minnesota it is said that the Norwegians sought the high ground, built their churches, settled their farms, and then left the rest of the countryside for others. St. Olaf College with its chapel on the bluff in Northfield is a well-known example of this, and there are many others.

The Gibbs farm, located in Falcon Heights, a small town five miles northwest of the Minnesota State Capitol in St. Paul, sits on some of the highest land in Ramsey County. The site can be seen in the movie *The Emigrants*. A small part of that elevation, roughly two blocks long from north to south and a block wide, reaches down from Falcon Heights into St. Anthony Park, a neighborhood in the northwest corner of St. Paul. The largest Lutheran seminary in the country sits like a crown on this inland promontory. Its main building, Bockman Hall, looks out over the cities of Minneapolis and St. Paul. Like the façade of the royal palace in Oslo, Norway, Bockman has three stories and columns with a Parthenon-like triangle above them, but Bockman is smaller. Each of its three floors has eighteen windows; each floor of the royal palace has twenty-one.

King Olaf V of Norway visited the seminary in May, 1968. Sagi and I went down and joined others from the neighborhood to welcome him when he arrived. At first, we mistook the King for Elmer L. Andersen, a former governor of Minnesota (1961-63), who lived three blocks away in a modern house that he and Mrs. Andersen had built.

The King got out of the car, waved to the crowd, and then walked past the library to Old Muskego Church, the first Norwegian church built in America. It was moved from Wisconsin to the seminary in the early 1900s. It sits in a small grove of evergreen trees, up a few steps from a path that links seminary faculty homes with one another.

After the King and his entourage disappeared inside the church, Sagi and I turned and went in the opposite direction, over to Bockman Hall. We climbed to the third floor, then made our way on to the roof of the building. We liked the view from there, especially in the late afternoon, when the setting sun made the Minneapolis skyline more dramatic than usual.

Most of the people who lived or worked in Bockman for any length of time probably knew how to get to the roof. It was not a secret. There were no signs forbidding it, but we preferred not to be observed because we had no official connection to the seminary; however, its library was our favorite place for reading away from home, and we knew the president and his wife. Their son Jim and I had lived across the hall from each other when we were in college.

I remember the day Jim was awarded a scholarship for two

years of graduate study in England. He came over, told my roommate and me about it, and said he was trying to locate his speech teacher, Lara Nilson. She had helped him prepare for the interview. He asked if either of us had seen her on campus that afternoon. We had not. Then he said he thought the interview had gone reasonably well. Years later we learned that, toward the end of it, one of the members of the committee had returned to the subject of Jim's being Lutheran. Why, the questioner wondered, is one Lutheran? Jim had been the star player on the college football team, and, at first, he thought of saying that if one's father is a football coach, there is a good chance one will grow up playing football, but instead of that, he said if his father had been a priest, he might have grown up Catholic. There was a pause. Jim maintained his presence of mind. There were no further questions.

Old Muskego Church, St. Paul

# Going Over the Unterberg
## (a picture book)

1    Sagi and her family were vacationing in Austria. It was 1973.

2    Sagi had been ill with chicken pox.

3    Now she was getting better, and the local doctor said it would soon be all right for her to go walking again.

4    All the guests at the country hotel on the edge of the Vienna Woods talked about hiking over the Unterberg.

5    Every day Sagi asked, "When can we go over the Unterberg?"

6    One day her father said, "The doctor says if you promise to tell me whenever you feel tired, we can go over the Unterberg tomorrow."

7    Sagi promised.

8    That evening they packed the things she would need for the hike.

9    Early the next morning, after a light breakfast, they started out.

10   First they came to the place along the stream where the Weinberg snails lived.

11    After that they passed the granite quarry.

12    They crossed the bridge where Sagi and her cousins often played Three Billy Goats Gruff.

13    The big meadow with its many alpine flowers was all around them.

14    The mountain was closer now.

15    There were more and more trees.

16    They dropped some leaves into what they called the "Schubert" brook and watched them float away.

17    Sagi was enjoying the hike.

18    They came to the World War II soldier's grave, marked only by a helmet on a stick.

19    Looking up, they could see the many switchbacks on the steepest part of the trail.

20    They began climbing.

21    Soon they left the forest behind them. There were no trees here, and the sun was bright.

22    They put on their hats and bandanas to protect themselves from sunburn.

23    Sagi's father said, "We will go more slowly now, half steps."

24    "When you are tired, I can carry you hook-a-pack, all the way to the top, if you want me to."

25    "From there we will be able to see the lodge in the distance."

26    After several switchbacks, when they were more than halfway up the rock face of the mountain, Sagi asked to be carried.

27    She was not a heavy child. She put her arms around her father and held on tightly so her weight centered on his shoulders. That made it easier for him.

28    They reached the last switchback.

29    Then they entered the forest at the top of the ridge and followed the trail that would take them, higher and higher, to the summit of the Unterberg.

30    They stopped at a lookout point for their midmorning snack.

31    In the valley far below, they could see Sagi's Aunt Renate hanging the wash out to dry on the clothesline at the old hunting lodge where she lived in the summer.

32    Sagi and her father drank some apple juice and ate nuts, raisins, and chocolate.

33    At midday they reached the inn near the top of the Unterberg.

34    There were a lot of people up there.

35    No one was as young as Sagi.

36    They ate lunch on the inn's terrace.

37    When they finished, Sagi's father made a big circle in the pebbles. He put an X where the hike had started. Then he showed her where they were at that moment and how they would get back down to the hotel.

38    After lunch they walked around the ski lift area.

39     They visited a small chapel and looked at the many faded paintings hanging on its walls.

40     In the early afternoon they started the long hike down the circle ridge that would take them back.

41     They crossed a stream filled with boulders and stayed away from the huge ant hill on their right.

42     When they came to a quiet pool in the stream, they stopped to look for the brown trout that lived there.

43     By this time it was getting dark.

44     When they arrived back at the hotel, dinner was over and done with.

45     The guests were having evening coffee on the terrace.

46     Some of them sat with shawls over their shoulders to protect themselves from the cool of the evening, just as Franz Schubert* had done when he visited Hainfeld farther down the valley in the early 1800s.

47     The hotel chef's wife kindly asked Sagi and her father if they wanted some soup.

48     Together they answered, "Yes, please," and sat down at a corner table not far from the water.

49     The lady from Amsterdam asked Sagi what she had done that day.

50     Sagi answered that she and her father had gone over the Unterberg.

---

* Austrian composer

51    The lady from Amsterdam did not believe her.

52    "You are only six years old," she said, "much too small to do
      that."

53    At that moment, Sagi's cousins came running up from the
      lodge.

54    They threw their arms around Sagi and hugged her, welcoming
      her back.

55    They knew she had gone over the Unterberg that day.

56    And that was all that mattered.

Courtesy J. Swenson

Mountain Stream

# The Piano

I.    Lessons

Everyone knew that Aunt Charlotte did not care if the grass was mowed or the car washed. The important things for her were that the piano was practiced and one's teeth were brushed. To take piano lessons or not to take them was a question that fell right in the middle of her "no discussion necessary" zone. I took piano lessons from the time I was in second grade until I left for college.

What other people thought and did was of no concern to Aunt Charlotte. Like Emily Dickinson, she formed a majority of one. Just mentioning that everybody was doing this or doing that (reading a book from the best-seller list was the worst) was enough to elicit what my uncle called her "predictable paroxysms of disapproval." Aunt Charlotte would look you in the eye and say, "But, my dear, that's what lemmings do."

I didn't have a lot of time to practice, but I never missed a lesson, and that was enough. By the time I was in high school, I could play hymns for church and songs that I heard on the radio, so

I thought it likely that if Sagi, too, would just go to her lessons, she would learn to play the piano well enough for her own enjoyment and that of others. No other exhortations would be needed.

Today, when I turn on the radio and hear someone playing a Bach prelude, a Chopin nocturne, or a Haydn sonata, I remember those composers' faces, as well as those of Beethoven, Schubert, Schumann and Mozart, because they were all on the covers of my practice books. Every springtime the fragrance of lilacs brings back memories of Mrs. Shore's pupils in their annual piano recital. It took place on a late and usually languid Sunday afternoon in May at the octagonal church with the stained-glass windows in the small Minnesota town where I lived when I was in grade school.

## II.    Teacher

When Sagi was seven, we began thinking about piano lessons. We had heard of Mrs. Marchand, a music teacher who lived a block away. We called, and she invited Sagi to her home for a lesson. The two of us walked over to the house together. It had a big, screened porch, and, after introductions, I asked Mrs. Marchand if she minded my waiting for Sagi out there. Permission was given. I had taken a book along.

Halfway through the lesson, Mrs. M. opened the door between her studio and the interior hall of the house. After that she opened a door between the hall and the vestibule. For the first time that afternoon, I could hear the piano. Sagi was playing a simple melody. Mrs. Marchand guided her through it several times until Sagi was able to play it easily. At that point something remarkable happened. While Sagi continued playing the melody, her teacher added a few notes of her own, not many, in the bass, sparingly, but, coming from the Steinway piano, the sound was rich, full, and interesting. I wanted to follow the line to see where it was going. I thought it was one of the most expressive and beautiful things I had ever heard emanate from a piano. For a moment I wondered if she had found the "lost" chord I remembered hearing about when I was just beginning the piano lesson journey. I knew at the time that Sagi was in good hands and that she, too, would remember this.

A year went by. There was a recital. By now Sagi knew several of the other pupils. One of them was Mattie, a girl the same age as Sagi. On the way home from the recital, Sagi asked me if I had liked the piece Mattie had played. I answered that I preferred the piece that she, Sagi, had played.

"Oh, good," she said, "I liked my piece, too, but Mattie said it was boring."

Remembering Aunt Charlotte, I said, "Maybe it's better not to pay too much attention to what other people say."

"Yes, it made me feel sad," said Sagi.

"Don't feel bad," I said, "I liked your piece. You did a good job, and I was proud of you."

We walked the rest of the way in silence. Neither of us mentioned it again.

III.    Pupil


Later that year Mattie came over to spend an afternoon at our house. We gathered in the sunroom between three and four o'clock to have hot fudge sundaes. I asked Mattie how she liked piano lessons.

"They're boring," she said. "Mrs. Marchand is old, and she's boring, too. I hate her. She makes me do the same old things over and over again. It's so boring."

I interrupted, "But isn't that the way we learn things, by doing them again and again, by practicing them? That's why people say 'Practice makes perfect.' "

"Repeating things is boring," said Mattie.

"Maybe Mrs. Marchand thinks you should learn one piece well before going on to another," I said. "What do you think about that?"

"I don't like the pieces she gives me, either," Mattie replied. "They're boring, too."

"Let's see if I've got this right," I said. "About this boring business, Mattie, what exactly does the word 'boring' mean to you? Can you help me understand that word a little better?"

"Well," she said, "boring means if I don't like something, then it is boring."

"So," I said, "you don't like repeating things, and you think your pieces are boring, but is there anything in particular about Mrs. Marchand's teaching that you don't like? Do you know what I mean?"

Mattie squinted, placed her chin heavily on the palm of her hand, shrugged, looked up at the sky outside the windows, and said, "Well, for one thing, she makes me use my left hand."

\* \* \* \* \* \* \*

When recital time came around the next year, I noticed Mattie was not there. After the program I asked Sagi, "Where was Mattie?"

"Oh," said Sagi, "she doesn't take piano lessons anymore. She quit."

"That's too bad," I said.

Sagi continued, "Mattie told me I should quit, too."

"What did you say to that?" I asked.

"You know the answer to that question," Sagi replied. "I told her I can't quit because, in our family, everybody takes piano lessons until they go away to college."

# Chicago

It's a long drive from the twin cities of Minneapolis and St. Paul, Minnesota, to Chicago, Illinois, Carl Sandburg's "city of the big shoulders." When Sagi was small, we used to break the trip into two parts. We would leave home in the early afternoon, drive for four solid hours, and arrive at the Edgewater Hotel in Madison, Wisconsin, in time for a late afternoon nap. When naptime was over, we'd go to dinner with our friends, Lauren and Dal. We liked the Edgewater. The staff knew how to bring just the right amount of drama to the serving of Cherries Jubilee; one never had to worry someone might set the table on fire. We enjoyed our visits there.

As the years passed, we sometimes took the train, but after arriving once in Chicago six hours late and almost missing an appointment with my tinnitus doctor out in Skokie, we decided that from then on we would fly.

By this time, Sagi liked airplanes. We never forgot the first time we saw a Boeing 747. It was parked with its nose as close as it could get to the huge windows of a gate area at O'Hare Airport. One had the impression it was trying to peek in to have a look at the people it would be taking nonstop to London.

Flying meant we would no longer stay at the Edgewater. We looked at brochures from Chicago hotels, and Sagi chose the Palmer House. Its lobby reminded her of the big room at Lake McDonald Lodge in Montana's Glacier National Park, and she thought the waiters in the Empire Room looked a little like park rangers.

As Sagi and I walked the few blocks from the Palmer House to the Art Institute, we saw Orchestra Hall. I told her about the time the Augustana Choir had sung there. The sixty singers assembled below stage level on a big hydraulic platform, and, promptly at eight o'clock, it was slowly raised into place. I don't think any of us ever forgot the moment when we came up out of a hole in the floor and saw the audience sitting out there in that resplendent space. I don't remember if our director, Dr. Arnold Running, chose to begin that concert with Francis Poulenc's *Mass in G*. The opening chords of the "Kyrie" would have been a good match for the grandeur of the hall.

The first painting Sagi and I saw as we entered the Art Institute was *Paris Street, Rainy Day, 1877* by Gustave Caillebotte. Its dimensions are approximately seven by nine feet. "Carl Sandburg would approve of this for the big city by the lake," I thought. Sagi was familiar with the painting from a picture of it in a card game we had at home, but she was surprised by how large it was. In the museum shop, we both bought postcards of our three or four favorite paintings. With the help of the Art Institute's map, we located them in the galleries and enjoyed seeing them "in person" for the first time.

Then we went back to the hotel. That was when I noticed there was no FM radio in our room.

After my time in the army, I lived in Chicago for two years. The only radio station I ever listened to was WFMT. In those days, members of the listening audience could subscribe to a monthly guide that listed the music that would be played hour by hour. WFMT was a commercial station, but the ads were read by the station's own announcers and never interrupted the programming. I considered this practice to be a good example of capitalism at its best, glaringly unlike the unbridled sort that has an unfortunate tendency to go awry every once in a while.

I had requested an FM radio when we reserved the room and had been told there would be one available. When I mentioned this at the front desk, they said there were no FM radios in the less expensive rooms. My heart sank. A day in Chicago without WFMT was, to my way of thinking, much worse than a day in Florida without orange juice. However, before I could say anything more, hotel personnel went on to say that all the rooms in the Palmer House Towers had FM radios, so, if we didn't mind moving up to a tower room for the same price as our present room, they would be happy to assist.

"No, we wouldn't mind at all," I said, and that's how we got into the habit of staying in the Palmer House Towers. In addition to the FM radio, there was a breakfast service. The next morning a triple-shelved trolley appeared. The waiter removed the many impeccably pressed white cloths, and the first things that appeared to

Sagi's wondering eyes were chocolate-covered doughnuts.

For someone like Sagi, who once asked her grandfather if Chocolate could be used as a name on a baptismal certificate, those doughnuts were a revelation. From that day to this, for Sagi and me, Chicago and chocolate have been a match.

Art Institute, Chicago

# Avalanche Creek Trail

Our friend Langseth and her Mercedes had the habit of executing U-turns in illegal and unlikely places. Going for a ride with her was like taking a trip into uncharted territory. One could never be certain of what might happen between one curve in the road and the next. For this reason, Langseth and her car were on Sagi's list of favorite things. Everyone likes pleasant surprises now and again – no one more than a child – and time spent with Langseth never failed to provide them.

The surprises came in a variety of forms, but they fell into three main categories: those that made us laugh out loud, the ones that left us chuckling, and the many that made us smile. Although we enjoyed them all, smiles were best because they were somehow easier to remember, and when we thought about them in solemn situations, there was less risk that we would embarrass ourselves, or people around us, with laughter.

More than thirty years have passed since that summer morning when we waited on the mountainside driveway for Langseth and her ivory car to appear. The car's name was Diva, but we were careful not to call her that unless we were sure she wasn't listening, or was out of earshot. Like all good divas, this one was temperamental. She refused to start in cold weather if her garage was not kept warm enough, and she didn't like heights. She would sputter and pout something dreadful if anyone dared ask her to go above the timber line. Diva was always easy to spot because the way Langseth drove her was rife with attitude, and, among the many Subarus and other practical cars one finds in Montana's Glacier National Park, the Mercedes stood out like a pair of five-inch heels in a closet filled with sensible shoes.

On that particular day, Diva was giving us a ride to Avalanche Creek, a few miles north of Lake McDonald Lodge. We had been to a park ranger program the week before at the campground. Ranger Bob had told us all about the terrible forest fire of 1910. He also reminded us that Glacier Park is home to many wild animals and that we, as visitors, must be aware that danger exists, even though much is done to make the park as safe as possible for those who visit it. Several other rangers took part in the program. We had seen Becky, the ranger who led our hike up to Sperry Glacier where we saw a grizzly bear – off in the distance – slide down a big snowbank. When it reached the bottom, it turned around, trudged back up, and slid down again. The grizzly did this several times. It was clear the bear was enjoying itself. When someone in the group asked Becky what we should do if the bear began moving over in our direction, Becky said, "First, you form a tight circle around me." Her words made us a little less anxious.

On the way to the campground parking lot, Langseth told us that, as far as she knew, no grizzly had ever been seen along Avalanche Creek. "But, of course," she added, "that's no guarantee there won't be one out there today." She also told about the time she was hiking to Granite Park Chalet. As she rounded a bend in the trail, she saw a mountain lion sauntering along ahead of her, gracefully flipping its tail back and forth, reminding her of an Englishman brandishing his umbrella.

It's often said there is no such thing as a bad hike in Glacier Park. Avalanche Creek trail is one of the best: it is short, a little over four miles up to the lake and back; the ascent is gradual, 500 feet, and it is close to water cascading over boulders and rocks. Trees provide shade all the way.

\* \* \* \* \* \* \*

When we emerge from the forest and see the sapphire blue lake in the middle of a vast bowl-shaped valley called a cirque, we are reminded, for a moment, of natural amphitheaters in Greece. Out under the sky at the far end of the lake, several streams tumble – almost fall – down the mountain and disappear into the lake.

We find a place to sit, open our Gokey's bag, and take out our lunch of apples, walnuts, and Hershey's chocolate. After eating, we rest for a while and then go exploring along the lake shore.

In midafternoon we start back down the trail to see how Diva is doing without us. Most of the time the path is wide enough to meet hikers coming up without breaking our stride. Hiking songs originated on trails like this one, but we are lost in thought until Langseth has had enough of quietude and begins conjugating Latin verbs out loud: I come, you come, it comes, and so on. Sagi joins in while I remember Caesar. This continues until we see a group of six or seven people coming toward us. They look as if they might be singing, but we can't hear anything over our Latin verbs. Even so, we can see they are mouthing something. As the hikers move closer to one another, then meet and pass by without slowing the pace, people in both groups hear what those in the other group are saying. When the hikers realize they are all conjugating Latin verbs, there are broad smiles all around, but no one misses a step. They just continue on their way.

Years later I tell this story to a friend of mine in Boulder. He is not surprised to hear it. "Oh, yes," he says, "I've been going to Glacier Park for as long as I can remember, and I've heard that story before. No one seems to know how the Latin thing got started. It must have been mentioned years ago – possibly in a book somewhere – and every once in a while people who've read it take the hike and decide to try out their Latin. Whatever the source, it does seem to happen, or it may simply be that the trail has that effect on people. But it's never French or Greek, it's always Latin."

# Gunsight Pass

One of the fire-engine red Glacier Park tour buses picked us up at Lake McDonald Lodge after breakfast. It took us over Logan Pass and stopped at Jackson Glacier Overlook. The driver pointed in the direction of Gunsight Pass and said, "There, that's where you want to go." About eight miles to the south we could see the notch that gave the pass its name. Sagi and I stepped off the bus and started out.

Today we were hiking to Sperry Chalet, four miles beyond Gunsight, to stay the night. We had made reservations months before. After walking several miles, we stopped for a hiker's snack, one appropriate for bear country.

Not long after that, as we left the valley and began the climb to the pass, the sky darkened. There was some rain, but we were dressed for it.

We reached an open area on a slope that was covered with compacted snow and ice. The trail led across it, a distance of some one hundred feet or more. Looking up to the left, beyond the snow, we could see water cascading down the mountainside until it tunneled its way into the ice bank and disappeared from view.

As we watched the rushing water, two young men dressed in full hiking gear made their way across the ice in our direction. As they went by, one of them said, "There's strong wind and heavy rain up ahead. We're turning back." Then he looked at Sagi and said, "Little girl, if you keep on going, there's a good chance the wind will blow you right off the mountain."

As he spoke, I noticed that some of the water from the swollen stream was backing up and beginning to flow over the snow bank, making the path even more treacherous. A lot of water was passing under the ice and snow that lay directly in front of us. Crossing that, I thought, presented a greater danger than any as yet unfelt wind and rain that might be headed our way. Stepping onto the snow-packed and increasingly icy path posed the risk of slipping and then going over the edge of the cliff, which was only a few yards away from where we were standing. It was also easy to imagine that a big chunk of what had become an ice bridge might suddenly break loose and be sent sailing over the lip of the precipice, like a Frisbee. Better not to be out there if that were to happen.

There weren't many people on the trail, but from the valley earlier that morning we had seen others up ahead of us. We waited. None of them were coming back. That bolstered our confidence. We decided the warning given by the two men had been a tad extreme.

We were from the Upper Midwest, a part of the country known for its violent and severe weather, so we had a proper respect for the forces of nature. Sagi and I had seen a tornado roar across our neighbors' rooftops, and when she was ten, we had been caught in a gale on the North Sea. More than once we had found ourselves in blizzards and cloudbursts. Now there was some lightning around, but it was not so scary as the strikes one sometimes witnesses in Chicago.

If bad went to worse, we would seek safety in breaks along the rock wall, stay there until the storm passed, and avoid being swept off the mountain. The way we reasoned it, not even a tornado could haul us out from small places between boulders, so we decided to go forward, even if that meant making a long detour.

Instead of venturing out on the snow and ice pack, we would keep our feet on solid ground. After scrambling up and going around, we would make our way back down again. The hike would be longer, but given the circumstances, we considered it to be the best choice.

We started crawling.

Sagi went first, just a few feet ahead of me. She was a considerate climber, always taking care not to dislodge too many small rocks in my direction. It took us a long time, but we made it. Shortly before we rejoined the trail, Sagi stopped, slowly turned to me and whispered, "Look, over there, blending in with the heather." I looked and saw first one and then several light-brown, white, and gray ptarmigan sitting off to the side, watching us, as though they were waiting for us to go by before continuing with whatever they had been doing before we appeared on the scene. Seeing them was special. Their muted colors were lovely. "They are our reward," Sagi said, "for taking the long way around."

Back on the trail, we saw that the sky on the other side of the pass was brightening. When we reached the stone hut at the top, we rested for a while, ate some chocolate, and then continued on our way. The storm was over. The sky was blue. From here, it was four or five miles to Sperry Chalet. The hiking was easier, even though we would soon be crossing the Continental Divide. We were in high mountain country. We saw bear grass and Indian paintbrush. In protected places, there were pasque flowers and blue gentians. To the left and far below us, we could see Lake Ellen Wilson glistening in the sun. To the right, up in the crags, we saw bighorn sheep, and there were goats in all directions.

We never forgot we were passing through bear country. We knew that aggressive behavior, like waving one's arms about, can sometimes keep black bears and mountain lions away, but that it was better to be quiet if one met a grizzly bear. The most important thing was not to surprise an animal, so we used the bear bells friends had given us. Some people we met said the sound didn't carry very far; others told us the sound would just arouse a bear's curiosity and bring it out to take a closer look at what was happening. We carried pepper spray with us and hoped we'd have the wit to use it adroitly if the need for it arose.

We knew before leaving the lodge that morning that there was an element of risk in what we were doing, but there is also danger in crossing streets. No one wants to stay on the same side of the street one's whole life long, so it's best if one learns to be careful.

We talked with one another, laughed, and sang songs. Not long after crossing the Continental Divide, we found ourselves at Sperry Chalet. We checked in, enjoyed a good dinner, and turned in early.

In the middle of the night I was awakened by a racket outside the room. I looked out the window and saw mountain goats clattering up and down the balcony along the side of the chalet. I didn't know if this was an unannounced nocturnal amusement for guests – provided by the National Park Service – or if someone, somewhere, had forgotten to close a gate.

Sperry Chalet, Montana

# Sledding

One January day, as Sagi and I were walking home from the post office, she saw some older children sledding on a steep slope in the park at the end of our street. She immediately wanted to try that for herself, so we went over to have a closer look. There were trees on both sides of the sledding path, and I had strong misgivings about allowing her to do this, but I said nothing.

Every year in late autumn the city parks department puts up orange plastic fencing in an attempt to keep youngsters from using that part of the park in winter. Just as regularly, someone takes the fencing down, rolls it up, and tries to hide it in the bushes farther along the hillside.

When we reached the jumping-off place, I suggested that we wait for a minute to see how the sledders negotiated what I considered to be a daunting drop from the sidewalk at the top to the almost flat playing field more than 100 yards below.

I noticed that those in charge were careful not to send a sled and its rider down until the area below was cleared. That was some comfort, but my concern about the trees could not be allayed.

There were several sleds in use. It took quite a while for riders to make their way back to the top of the hill. They had to go far out of the way to use a path that provided a gradual and less slippery ascent to the top. The sledders didn't move along too quickly, but they moved, and soon I noticed Sagi making her way, slowly but surely, to the head of the line.

As I waited for her turn to come, I had plenty of time to consider the arguments for and against allowing her to do this. Trying not to be too alarmist, I pointed out the danger posed by the trees, but I sensed that her mind was made up. I knew I had a tendency to be overprotective, but, at the same time, I was reluctant to step in and put the kibosh on it. I didn't want her to lose face with children from the neighborhood.

When it was Sagi's turn, others held the sled and waited until she was comfortably seated. Then she signaled that she was ready. No push was needed because, at the start of the slope, the path pointed almost straight down. I held my breath and then, in seconds, it was over. The sled flew down the hill and came slowly to a halt. Those who'd gone before helped Sagi stand up. She turned around, looked in my direction, and waved. I could see how pleased she was. Her smile seemed to reach from ear to ear. She was happy, and I was, too, but I was even happier when she said she was ready to go home.

# Pastrami

When I was in the army in the early 1960s, years before Sagi was born, I was stationed at Fort Holabird, Maryland, on Chesapeake Bay, between Washington, D.C., and Baltimore. On weekends, army buddies and I took the train to New York City. The first thing we did after arriving at Penn Station was walk to Carnegie Deli at West 55th Street and Seventh Avenue for pastrami sandwiches.

After my army days were over, I missed the city and its good pastrami sandwiches. Back in Minnesota, I stopped eating sandwiches and settled instead for bagels. They weren't as good as New York City bagels, but they were better than no reminder at all of visits to Manhattan.

When Sagi was in graduate school in the 1990s, I visited New York City often and always stayed with friends on West 71st Street who bought their pastrami at Zabar's on Broadway. Thirty years had passed, but New York pastrami was still the best.

Pastrami is a Yiddish word, taken from the Romanian word *păstra*, which means "to preserve." There are several ways to preserve pastrami, chief among them curing, pickling, and smoking.

Pastrami is usually highly seasoned, most often including caraway and coriander.

Before pastrami crossed the Atlantic Ocean to America, it was found in Eurasia, especially in the region around the Black Sea, where, even today, cattle are scarce. The people there used lambs, goats, and even geese to make their pastrami.

Beef is the American contribution to pastrami. In the late nineteenth century, immigrants from eastern Europe were arriving here in large numbers. They began using beef. It must have been an improvement because it soon became one of the great food favorites for New Yorkers. Often served with mustard, coleslaw, horseradish, or egg omelets, it is as popular today as ever.

\* \* \* \* \* \* \*

In 1975 we visited Tanglewood, the summer music home of the Boston Symphony, located in the Berkshire Hills of western Massachusetts. It was almost noon when we arrived. I went to check out the restaurant. Sagi said she would meet me there later, after she finished exploring the place where Nathaniel Hawthorne wrote *Tanglewood Tales*.

When I saw pastrami on the menu, memories of my army days – all the long discussions about pastrami – came flooding back: cured or uncured, Dijon mustard or horseradish, flank steak or brisket, kosher or non-kosher, rye bread or pumpernickel. There would be a lot to talk about at lunch.

Just as I turned around to look for Sagi, she came running up and said, "Daddy, come and see. Leonard Bernstein is conducting the student orchestra over there in the shed, and he forgot to put his shirt on."

TIMED BY
BENRUS

Penn Station Clock, New York City

# Smith Square, London

The usher looked at Sagi, who was almost ten, and said, "You will enjoy the concert more if you can see the expressions on the musicians' faces." He showed us to seats in the second row, right side, and asked, "How will this do?" "Very well, thank you," I replied. "You're welcome," he said, "enjoy the concert."

We were at St. John's, Smith Square, in London for a chamber music concert that was to be broadcast by the BBC. The host asked the audience not to forget that the recording equipment picked up all sounds; for that reason, it was requested that we try to be as quiet as possible. The members of the string quartet took their places while the sound engineers finished arranging the microphones.

After we were seated, Sagi asked, "Is this a church?"

"Not anymore," I answered. "It was a church for a long time, but it has been deconsecrated, and now it is used mostly for musical events of one kind or another."

"What does deconsecrated mean?" Sagi continued.

"St. John's no longer functions officially as a church," I said. "It has lost that right."

"Is that like losing your driver's license?" Sagi asked.

"Something like that," I said, "yes."

When Sagi noticed that one of the pieces to be performed was Franz Schubert's *Death and the Maiden*, she wondered if Schubert had written any music about death and the boy.

"Yes, he did," I said, and asked if she remembered my reading a poem called *The Erlking*. "Schubert set that poem to music," I added, "and we have a recording of it sung by Hans Hotter."

"What is it about?" Sagi asked, "I don't remember."

"It tells the story of a father and son riding horseback in the dark of night. It's windy; the trees are casting spooky shadows; leaves are blowing around, and the little boy is afraid, remember?"

"That one is scary," said Sagi.

"Yes, it is," I agreed. "That's why we haven't listened to it very often."

"Will it be scary today?" she asked.

"No," I answered, "today is all music, no words. It won't be scary."

"Why did Schubert write about death?" Sagi asked.

"I don't know why he did that," I answered, "but in those days people didn't live to be as old as they do today. Schubert died when he was thirty-one. He wrote *Death and the Maiden* when he was twenty-six. Maybe he had some reason for thinking about death. I don't know."

After a while Sagi said, "I'm hungry." I told her there would be a reception downstairs when the program was over. "Are we going?" she wanted to know.

"Yes, we are," I replied. "There will be good things for you to eat, don't worry."

After the concert there was champagne for the adults and pear juice for the children. For everyone there was smoked Scottish salmon and sliced cucumbers on thin pieces of rye bread.

When the reception concluded, we went outside to wait for our friend Rosemary to take us back to her family's home in Cobham for dinner. Sagi looked around the square, then at St. John's in the middle of it, and said, "It doesn't look like a church. It has four towers, one on each corner, and they're all alike. I've never seen a church like that."

"You're right," I said, "but there's a story that explains why the four towers are the same. Rosemary told me. Would you like to hear it?"

"Yes," she said, so I began.

"St. John's is a Baroque church. It was built a long time ago, in 1728, by a famous architect whose name was Thomas Archer. You know St. Agnes Catholic Church in St. Paul, with the onion dome, where we went with Ingeborg, the lady from the German Consulate in Chicago. St. Agnes is also Baroque, but it was built almost two hundred years later, in the early 1900s. It is a faithful copy from original plans for Baroque churches in Austria."

"But why does St. John's have four towers and no onion dome?" asked Sagi.

I continued, "Anne was Queen of England from 1702 until her death in 1714. On the day Mr. Archer went to speak with her about what St. John's should look like, it seems he disagreed with her about something. Queen Anne was vexed. She kicked over her footstool so that its four legs pointed straight up in the air. She looked at it for a moment, and then she said, 'There, Mr. Archer, build it like that,' and he did. That's why some people, even today, call St. John's 'Queen Anne's Footstool.' "

British flag

# Sissinghurst

Sissinghurst makes visible the forged genius of its owners, Vita Sackville-West and her husband, Sir Harold Nicolson. It is the story of how two strong personalities worked together to create an aesthetic that transcended their different temperaments and resulted in something that surpassed what they might have achieved had they worked alone.

England is known for its cottage gardens, where unseen weeders labor among exuberant – sometimes almost riotous – mounds of flowers that seem always ready and waiting to have their close-ups taken for next year's calendars. France, on the other hand, is famous for severe lines, whether in the clipped shrubs that stretch into the distance of its grand and formal gardens, or in the rows of vegetables that can be found in the humblest of its kitchen gardens. Geometric spareness and restraint are valued hallmarks there.

A good partnership builds on the strengths of those who form it. Nicolson was an advocate of the straight line. Sackville-West preferred lines that were sinuous and supple. Sissinghurst itself, a ruin when they found it, provided the means for reconciling these two divergent views. Its many brick walls played an important part in determining what would happen there. Although they placed constraints on both Nicolson and Sackville-West, the walls also enabled them to experience the heady freedom that comes from having to create within the confines of an existing framework. Like thoughtful people in any field of endeavor, they were not graceless when it came to exercising their authority. The site was allowed to speak for itself, and it helped to mold what was done there.

Walls treat all lines, whether straight or curved, alike. They block them. Nicolson expended a lot of effort finding the places where straight lines could be fashioned. This struggle rendered his decisions more discerning and enhanced the garden as a whole. It fused what he and his wife were doing with what had been there for centuries, thereby, like a fortuitous act of providence, ennobling it with an integrity and a spirit that leave one with the impression that the garden is older than it is in actual fact. While Nicolson drew the lines that gave the garden its unity and coherence, Sackville-West planted in the defined spaces that resulted. Much of what she created continues to be regarded today as inspired.

A famous composer was once asked what it is that makes a pianist great. He answered that there is more to playing the piano than just hitting the right notes. A fine pianist, he believed, understands the spaces between the notes.

Sackville-West's gift, nourished and honed from childhood on, was that she understood what to do with the spaces between the brick walls and the paths. She filled them with romantic abundance, but thanks to the strength of the garden's plan, its "bones," Sissinghurst became a model of balance, proportion, and harmony.

Its location is unprepossessing: the garden sits on a few acres of downward-sloping land. There are no grand vistas like those conjured up by Capability Brown.* Although Sissinghurst is in Kent, the "Garden of England," the surrounding countryside does not immediately draw one's attention. With the exception of the tower, the buildings which Nicolson and Sackville-West found at Sissinghurst are nondescript and cannot be said to sit well on the property. It took a lot of work to make this into the beautiful place it is today.

Sissinghurst is a tribute to the accomplishment of two remarkable people. Sagi was nine years old when we visited there. As we were leaving, I asked her what she had liked best about the garden and what she thought she would remember longest. I hoped she would mention an avenue of small trees, the white garden, or the vegetable garden, but instead she told me she had heard someone say that when Sackville-West died, her family found she did not have a nice dress to wear for her funeral.

---

* English landscape architect, 1715 – 1783

Versailles, France

# The Lady from Amsterdam
## (a true story in an imagined setting)

We had seen her before on the hotel's motor launch. She had given Sagi a brochure for a yodeling festival that was to be held in a village on the other side of the lake. We decided to go.

A week later, as we sat on the rickety wooden benches, the lady from Amsterdam came on board and sat down beside us. She placed her open satchel between herself and Sagi, announced her name, and began talking. As the weathered vessel pulled away from the dock, picking up speed and plunging through one wave after another, the bag tipped over in Sagi's direction, and its contents slowly spilled out. The lady from Amsterdam seemed oblivious to what was happening and went right on talking. She asked for our name and wanted to know where we were from. When I gave her our surname, she said, "Oh, that is a Dutch name. Are you Dutch?" I told her my paternal grandparents left Holland for America in the late 1800s, when they were children.

"That's interesting," she said, as the launch continued making its way across the rough water, and more and more items emerged from her handbag. "I might be sitting where you are today, except for the fact that my grandparents stayed behind when all their siblings and their children – my aunts and uncles – left for the United States. No, my grandparents didn't go. Someone had to look after their parents and tend the farm."

She wanted to know what state we were from. Trying not to look at the gaping bag and the effect this was having on Sagi, I responded by saying there are some cities and towns in our part of the country where the Dutch inhabitants still scrub the streets in springtime, when the tulips are in bloom.

"Please go on," she said.

"When I was a boy," I continued, "our nearest neighbors were families with names like Ebeling and Ennenga. All the lawns and gardens were enclosed by hedges."

By now I could see a camera, a polka dot scarf, an address book, and other things that women of a certain age are wont to carry about with them. Even with all this going on around her, the lady from Amsterdam seemed to take no notice.

What was my school like, she wanted to know. I said there were paintings of tulips, windmills, and wooden shoes on the walls, and the teacher read us the story of Hans Brinker, who skated on the frozen canals in winter.

"Oh, yes," said the lady from Amsterdam, "those were the good old days in Holland. Things have changed a lot since then, and they won't be changing back anytime soon."

Then she looked out toward the village on the far shore.

We were in the middle of the lake now, and the water was choppy. At that moment, I saw Sagi grab for something as it was about to roll off the bench onto the muddy floor. She managed to catch what looked to me like a bamboo chopstick. The lady from Amsterdam saw it, too. She turned, snatched it away from Sagi and said, kindly, "No, my precious, you don't want to play with that."

Then she held the stick away from us, pressed a button release at its base, and, to our amazement, a long, narrow stiletto blade popped from its carrier.

"Do you know what this is?" she asked us. We shook our heads left and right. "This is what little old ladies like me carry around with them for their own protection in Amsterdam. I never leave my house without it. It has made itself useful several times."

We received this information in silence, as did those who were sitting near us. Then she returned the blade to its carrier, put it in a zippered pocket, and added, "No, Holland is not just about tulips, windmills, and wooden shoes – not anymore."

Swiss Lake

# Agatha Christie

"Trust me, Mr. E., Sagi will like them, and so will you." It was Ken speaking, a ninth-grader who lived a few blocks away. He was talking about the four black-and-white Agatha Christie movies made in England during the 1960s. They were being shown downtown at the St. Paul Arts and Sciences Center. They starred the inimitable British actress Margaret Rutherford as Miss Marple. I had never heard of her.

"Have you seen all four of them?" I asked.

"More than once," he answered. "They show them every year on Saturday nights beginning in late January."

"How long has this been going on?" I asked.

"Oh, I don't know exactly – two, maybe three years," he said.

"Agatha Christie wrote murder mysteries, didn't she?" I asked. "Someone has to die in these movies, right?"

"Right," he said, "but don't worry, it's murder 'lite.' As I said, try it, you'll like it."

I had reservations about murder being treated lightly, especially in films seen by preadolescents, but I trusted Ken's judgment and that of his family, so, when Saturday night came, we went.

We didn't watch a lot of television, and going out to a movie was not something we did very often, but after seeing *Murder at the Gallop*, we knew that our next three Saturday nights would find us at the movies.

For the next few years we went to see them, always arriving early – shortly after seven o'clock – and always taking the same seats. Years later, we were still able to carry on little conversations that consisted mostly of lines taken from those four films.

Even today, when one of us expresses hopes for something the other considers unlikely, the response will often be, "Those hopes must sustain you." Or, when one of us enters a room that is clearly in full-blown disaster mode, one might hear, "What, a child (or parent) of mine, living in a place like this?" And if someone is a bit abrupt, the ensuing muttering might run along the lines of, "I say, he (or she) is a bit on the brisk side this morning, eh, what?"

When Sagi was in high school, we saw the four Agatha Christie color movies from the 1970s. Our favorite was *Death on the Nile*. Margaret Rutherford was not in it. She died in 1972, eighty years and eleven days after her birthday, May 11, 1892. We missed her.

Our favorite scene in *Death on the Nile* was the one in which Angela Lansbury and David Niven dance the tango. From that time on, whenever we heard a tango on the radio at home, we would do our own version of that dance, from one end of the living room to the other and back again, thus paying homage to Ms. Lansbury and Mr. Niven for their beguiling and unforgettable performance. As far as we were concerned, it wasn't nearly long enough.

We missed seeing Agatha Christie's play *The Mousetrap* when we were in London in 1976, but the next year, in San Francisco, we saw it in a small theater not far from Union Square.

Sagi became a fan of Agatha Christie and an avid reader of her books. One day when I met her after school, she said the Scholastic Aptitude Test coordinator had told the class that all the words on the SAT tests appear somewhere in Christie's books. The message was clear: for those interested in trying to ace the vocabulary part of the SAT, all they had to do was study the dozens of Christie mysteries. By the time Sagi took the SATs, she had finished all of them.

# Fairmont Hotel, San Francisco

We stopped in San Francisco on our way to visit friends who were staying at Asilomar on the Monterey Peninsula, two hours south of the city on the bay.

No sooner had we walked into Union Square than Sagi looked up and saw the glass-walled elevator on the east side of the Fairmont. She turned to me and said, "Oh, let's go for a ride in that elevator." So much for Union Square.

As the elevator rose sedately and climbed the side of the hotel, Sagi stood with her hands pressed against the glass wall opposite the elevator door. Looking out and down, she exclaimed, "Oh, the earth is falling away!"

She did not turn around to see that I, not one for heights, was studying the shine on my shoes.

Golden Gate Bridge

# Pastures of Heaven

"How much farther is it?" Sagi asked.

"About thirty miles," I answered.

It was 1977. We were on the way from Saratoga to visit my college housemate Bruce and his family. They were visiting relatives who lived in what John Steinbeck called the "pastures of heaven," a low range of mountain hilltops that lies between Monterey and Salinas, in California.

"Where are we now?" Sagi asked.

"We're getting close to Salinas," I replied. "We'll change roads there and take something smaller that will be more interesting for you. You can start looking for signs that say Monterey. Maybe you'll see one for the Monterey Peninsula as well."

"Why is everything so flat around here?" Sagi continued.

I said, "There have to be some flat places in the world so farmers can grow food for us to eat. If their fields were on hills, their tractors would tip over, and we would all go hungry."

Sagi's response to this was, "We could eat vegetables from our garden."

"Yes," I said, "that's true, but not everyone has a vegetable garden."

"We could share with them."

"Right again."

"Oh, look," she said, "there's a sign for Monterey."

We left Highway 101 and headed west.

"What's that growing in those fields?" Sagi wanted to know. "Is that lettuce?"

"No," I said, "there are lettuce fields around here somewhere, but those are artichokes."

"Can people choke on artichokes?" Sagi asked, and then she laughed to herself. I looked over at this little girl, smiled, and patted her on the shoulder. She smiled back. She didn't like car trips, but she was making the best of it.

"How lucky I am," I thought. Sometimes I felt that without her I would float off into the stratosphere and be lost forever. She was the mooring line that connected me to everything on earth.

"Do you know why there's a 'choke' in 'artichoke'?" I asked.

"No, I don't," she said. "Why?"

"Because there really is a part of the artichoke that's called the 'choke'," I said.

"Where is it?" she wanted to know. "Can you see it?"

"Yes, one can," I said.

"Can we stop right now and look at it?" she asked.

"Yes, if you'd like to."

"I would like to," she said. "Please. Will the farmer mind?"

"No, I don't think so," I said. We turned off the road into a field driveway.

"This is fun," said Sagi. When the car stopped, she hopped out and ran to the edge of the field. I followed, and we looked at the artichokes together.

"They're pretty," she said.

"Yes, they are," I agreed.

"But they are hard to eat," she added.

"It takes some practice," I told her.

"May I take one home with me?"

"Yes," I said, "we'll find a store and buy one."

"Where do artichokes come from?" Sagi continued.

"Artichokes are part of the thistle family. The scale-like leaves are called bracts. You can tell whether an artichoke is fresh or not by taking a bract and bending it back; if it snaps off close to the base that means the artichoke is fresh. When you take all the bracts away, you will be left with just the choke. It's called that because it really can choke a person."

Sagi looked at the artichokes more carefully. "Artichokes grow on stems, the way pineapples do," she observed.

"Yes, they do," I said. "Do you know pineapples are a symbol of hospitality? Some people have stone or concrete pineapples mounted on their gateposts. You've seen them in places like Wayzata and Winnetka, remember? A pineapple on the gatepost is a way of saying 'welcome' to the guests who come to your house."

"Would an artichoke on someone's gatepost mean he's planning to choke them?" she asked.

"I don't know," I answered, "but it might be a good idea to stay away from gateposts that have artichokes on them."

"There were gateposts at the Villa Montalvo. Did they have pineapples on them?" Sagi went on.

"No," I said, "they didn't. I think those were griffins."

"It would be good in a murder mystery if the murderer had artichokes on his gateposts," she said. "Agatha Christie could figure out who the murderer was by knowing that."

"Or," I added, "it could be a tip-off for visitors."

"Yes," said Sagi.

"Maybe you can pass that information along to Ms. Christie some day," I suggested.

"Oh, Agatha Christie died last year," said Sagi. "Don't you remember?"

She wanted to know if there would be gateposts at the house we were going to visit.

"Yes," I said, "it's a big place. Bruce says his in-laws plan to sell the house to the Holiday Inn Company when they retire. It has an electric gate, speaking of which, we had better be on our way. We don't want to be late at the gate."

We continued driving west toward Monterey until we saw the sign saying "Jorundgard Grade, Private Road." Bruce said we have to check in at the gatehouse, and when we get closer to the main house, the gate will open automatically.

We turned off to the left and stopped when the guard stepped out into the road. They were expecting us. We began the drive up the mountain. There were other houses along the way. As we neared the top, we saw the gate. The road beyond it curved around the hill to the right and disappeared from view. We couldn't see any evidence of a house or people. We slowed down as we approached the gate. When we were about a driveway's length away, it opened, slowly, like magic. We drove through without stopping, and it closed itself behind us.

Estate Gate

# Brahms Piano Duet

Every year the Minnesota Music Teachers Association sponsors a contest for piano students. The winners are invited to perform in Northrop Auditorium at the University of Minnesota. The Schmitt Music Company fills the big stage with pianos. One category at a time, the students take their places at the pianos, and together they play the piece they've been practicing alone for the past several months. For students and audience members alike, it is a special event, an occasion to remember.

Sagi had learned the treble part of a Brahms piano duet and was one of the winners. The final practice was scheduled to take place at the Schmitt Music store in Brooklyn Center a week before the concert in Northrop.

We did not have a car at that time, so Sagi and I walked over to her piano teacher's house to ride with others who were going to the rehearsal. Our ride never arrived, so Mrs. Marchand's husband took us out to Brookdale Mall. When we reached it, he stopped the car, pointed to the mall entrance and said, "Here it is." We got out of the car, and he drove away. We looked for Schmitt Music, but it was nowhere to be seen. I asked a passerby for directions, and she said, "You are in the wrong place; it's over there." She pointed in the direction of some buildings that were on the other side of a faraway freeway. I had no billfold with me, and cell phones weren't yet in widespread use. If Sagi missed the practice, she might not be allowed to take part in the concert at Northrop.

There was nothing else to be done; we would have to walk. I looked around and saw a water overflow channel made of concrete. It was dry as a bone. There wasn't a cloud in the sky, and we didn't think there was a dam nearby that could open up and release tons of water in our direction. The area was not fenced, so, even if water had suddenly appeared, we still had the option of walking out of the channel and onto a highway. I looked for a "No Trespassing" sign, but didn't see one. We left the sidewalk and started out. I didn't think it was too far, but it was farther than I thought. The walking was relatively easy, but the environment was harsh and inhospitable. We passed beneath highways, streets, and railroads. At times the surrounding landscape was so bleak it reminded me of desolate scenes in New Wave films, but the walking itself didn't bother us. We continued on our way.

The channel led almost directly to the buildings that had been pointed out to us. We could see the Schmitt Music sign on one of them. We reached the frontage road, climbed out of the channel, walked a block or two to the west, and entered the music store. There was a big room with many pianos in it. The rehearsal was in progress.

We must have been a little late, but no one mentioned it. One of the teachers in charge showed Sagi to her assigned piano. Sagi sat down on the bench next to her duet partner and began playing together with the others. I found a chair and thanked my lucky stars there had not been a cloudburst.

When the practice session was over, I stood up, and there was Judy Hanson. We had been friends since grade school, but had not seen one another for years. After a moment, I asked, "Do you have someone playing here today?"

"Oh, yes," she said, "my daughter, Jane; she's sitting over there on the piano bench talking to her duet partner, the girl with the auburn hair."

"That girl," I said, "is my daughter, Sagi."

\* \* \* \* \* \* \*

A week later, Jane and Sagi sat on the Northrop stage with the other winners. Sagi and I had taken the free intercampus bus from St. Paul over to the Minneapolis campus. Once again, I was not carrying any money. Judy noticed my predicament, smiled her signature smile, and lent me the price of admission. I remember her saying, as she took the cash from her purse and gave it to me, "There, that's money I'll probably never see again," but she did.

# The U of M, St. Paul

I.    University Grove

It doesn't much concern those of us who live in the Twin-City metro area, but most of St. Paul, in terms of feet above sea level, is higher than Minneapolis.  Once in a while, residents of University Grove, a Falcon Heights neighborhood on the north side of the northwest corner of St. Paul, will say their part of town includes the highest point in Ramsey County.  But, for most Twin Citians, matters pertaining to elevation are of little interest; however, there are some exceptions.

The people who decided where to lay the railroad tracks and where to build the streetcar lines did pay attention to elevation. When the streetcar line was constructed between the University of Minnesota main campus in Minneapolis and the farm campus in St. Paul, huge earthmovers cut a trench through the hill on the north side of University Grove, making it easier for the streetcars to negotiate the grade between the two campuses.

As the years went by, architect-designed houses were built

in University Grove between Hoyt Avenue on the south (the border between St. Paul and Falcon Heights) and the streetcar cut on the north. The east border of University Grove is Cleveland Avenue; the west border is Fulham Street. The Grove is six blocks long east to west and one block wide. Before World War II, the university built a golf course on the north side of the streetcar track. The intercampus streetcars were replaced by buses in 1954, but it is still possible today to walk the path that follows the old streetcar right-of-way. It is an amenity for the neighborhood, a tangle of brush and small trees that passes through a residential part of town. Some of the railroad ties that anchored the streetcar rails are still visible in their original places. Walkers have to take care not to stumble over them.

II.    *Harriet the Spy*

Children have played in the woods that border the southwest edge of the University of Minnesota golf course for decades, building forts, tree houses, and dirt-bike paths. The summer when Sagi and her friend Sally finished reading Louise Fitzhugh's *Harriet the Spy*, they decided it was time for them, like Harriet, to pay more careful attention to what goes on around them. Like scientists on the nearby campus, they armed themselves with pens and notebooks, staked out a "research plot" on the golf course, and began writing down everything that transpired within it. Not wanting to cause comment and run the risk of compromising the integrity of their observations, it was deemed necessary for the observers to stay out of sight of those whom they observed. The tenth hole, with its sand trap close to the woods, was perfectly suited to this purpose.

For most of that summer the two girls spent several hours every day engaged in this activity. I went along to serve as their lookout and spent most of my time well away from them and the sand trap. I sat on one of the thirty-five concrete steps that lead down from the professors' houses in the Grove to the abandoned streetcar stop below.

Research, as anyone knows who has ever engaged in it, can grow tedious at times; when this happens, a researcher needs to take a break. When no one was in sight, Sagi and Sally passed the time making little roads and patterns in the sand trap with the palms of their hands. When golfers came into view, the girls quickly returned to their observation posts in the woods while I raked and restored the sand to the way it had been before we arrived on the scene.

In my opinion, we always left the sand nicer than it was when we found it; we kept it clean and free of fur balls, dead birds, and other debris that one finds in a forest environment.

One day in early August, the observers saw something different from anything they had seen before. A man came out of the club house a block away and across the street from the sand trap. He headed straight in their direction. The path he took did not match any of those made by previous subjects, and he was moving at a pace that was definitely faster than that of the ordinary golfer. Sagi and Sally also noted that he was not carrying a golf club, nor was he toting a golf bag. This constituted highly unusual behavior. It alarmed the observers. They called for outside support. I stood up, walked over, made sure the sand was neat, and then we waited.

The groundsman came up and introduced himself. We did the same. He was not impressed by what we were doing with his sand. He asked us to please refrain from using the sand trap in the future. Silently, we pledged to obey his request. Never again would we disfigure, disrupt, disturb or dis- in any way anything having to do with his sand trap.

From now on, like good researchers everywhere, whenever there was a lull in the work, we would go somewhere off-site and have a coffee, or a lemonade.

Ryōan-ji, Kyoto

# Ryōan-ji, Kyoto

I saw the Pacific Ocean for the first time when I was ten years old. I remembered this as Sagi and I drove from San Mateo over the ridge to Half Moon Bay, and then north along the ocean to San Francisco. We were on our way to have tea at the Japanese Garden in Golden Gate Park, but first I wanted Sagi to see the Golden Gate Bridge. I asked her to close her eyes until we arrived at the California Palace of the Legion of Honor, the museum that overlooks the Golden Gate and enjoys an unforgettable view of the bridge. I parked the car and helped Sagi, her eyes still closed, to the overlook. When she was facing in the direction of the bridge, I said, "Now you can open your eyes." She still remembers seeing the bridge for the first time.

From there we drove to the Japanese Garden, walked in, crossed over the steep footbridge, and had tea.

I had told Sagi about Ryōan-ji, one of several famous gardens in Kyoto, Japan. There was a picture of it in my elementary school encyclopedia. It was one of my favorite things. Frank Lloyd Wright's "Fallingwater" house in Pennsylvania was another. I spent a lot of time looking at these two photographs.

The first time I visited Japan, I went directly to Kyoto. I stayed at Mrs. Thani's guesthouse because it was only a few blocks from Ryōan-ji. I walked to the garden every day, paid the admission, and looked around the gift shop, hoping to find a black-and-white photo of the garden that would be something like the one I remembered from grade school. I did this every morning for more than a week, but never found what I was looking for. There were many pictures of the garden, but they were all in color. Not one of them was taken from the angle I wanted. I never bought anything in the shop, but I always took the time to look.

The garden is composed of rocks of different shapes and sizes, arranged in a thirty-three by one hundred-foot rectangle of raked lag gravel. There is a viewing platform along one side of the garden, and every day I walked up and down the full length of it, stopping now and then, until I was ready to sit down for a while at my usual place. It was not a festival time of year. I always went early in the morning and never saw anyone else there.

But one day I heard a rustling sound behind me. I turned and saw a monk approaching. He was wearing long traditional robes. His arms were crossed and his hands were covered by folds in the robe. I stood up to face him. When he was quite close to me, he stopped and bowed, very slowly, from the waist. I did the same. He bowed several times. So did I. Then he let one hand drop to his side and extended the other in my direction. I saw that he was holding something wrapped in wrinkled paper that had yellowed around the edges. He wanted to give this to me. At first I shook my head no, but then I accepted it. He bowed again. I bowed, too. Then he motioned for me to open the packet. I undid the dry, crinkly paper and saw the same picture I remembered seeing years ago in the *Encyclopedia Britannica*. I didn't know what to say.

It was clear that he understood my surprise. There were several other postcards in the package. I took the time to look at all of them. When I finished, I carefully put them back in the yellowed envelope and held it out to this monk who had appeared out of nowhere. He shook his head from side to side and kept his arms folded. I held the little package to my chin, trying to indicate how special this was to me. I could see he understood my meaning. When he refused to take it back, I reached for my wallet. As soon as he saw what I was about to do, he closed his eyes and moved his head slowly from left to right. I was at a loss as to what I should try next. He saw my confusion, then smiled, bowed to me one last time, turned and was gone.

Although I continued going to Ryōan-ji every day for the rest of my time in Kyoto, I never saw him again.

Today this photo is framed and hangs next to the fireplace in my condo. When I stop to consider the astonishments I have known in my lifetime, this gift is always among them.

Courtesy P. O'Toole

Stone Fireplace

# Rum Baba

It is said that Count Stanislaus Leszczynski (1677–1766) brought the recipe for baba from Poland to France, and that it was his idea to combine it with rum. The baba is a cake leavened with yeast. Working with it is challenging. That is why babas are not usually made at home.

A rum baba is not as dense as pound cake and not as light as a cream puff. Its texture is less uniform than that of sponge cake, but, like sponge cake, it should hold its shape. Although they can be made in muffin tins, rum babas are usually baked in individual cylindrical molds.

Rum babas, cupcakes, and muffins are all round, but rum babas can be more than twice as high as cupcakes and muffins. Their distinctive shape is reminiscent of the long full skirts that many old women wear in Slavic countries. Baba is the word for "old woman" in Polish.

An absolute requirement for a rum baba is rum – the finer the rum, the better the baba. Some establishments offer a choice of rums. This can become expensive.

When the baba is served, it is cut lengthwise in half and presented flat sides up. How much rum to add is a matter of personal preference. A sprinkling of rum is enough for most people. Some restraint is called for. The plate should not be wet with rum. Better to keep it subtle.

An apricot glaze with a hint of lemon may be added.

There is also the matter of raisins. Rum babas do not need raisins, but if you want to include them, they should be marinated in rum for a day or two, the way raisins are marinated in Malaga wine for the Viennese dessert called Sicilienne.

Sagi and I ate our first memorable rum babas at the Pâtisserie Boisière in Carmel, California, more than thirty years ago. They have been part of life's adventure ever since. My favorite place for rum babas in Paris is Le Train Bleu restaurant at the Gare de Lyon. In New York City the babas were always outstanding at Alain Ducasse in the Essex House on Central Park South.

# Limerick

I was surprised one day when Sagi announced that someone was sponsoring a limerick contest at school, and that she was planning to enter it. "Now all I have to do," she said, "is come up with an idea."

I said, "That's great, go for it," and then went back to whatever it was that I'd been working on.

At dinner that evening we tried to come up with something that might be helpful to her, but, as far as I can recall, our efforts were not exactly crowned with success. After a day or two, Sagi's enthusiasm started to show some promise. I could see that she was serious about it. For a week the house was filled with the sound of limericks, some of them raucous. At last the day arrived for turning them in. I remember wishing her well as she went off to school that morning.

When Sagi arrived home that afternoon, she stopped at my door to say the winners would be announced the next day at an all-school forum.

"Good," I said.

"Do you want to hear my limerick?" she asked.

"But of course," I replied.

She smiled. I could tell she had come up with something that was going to give the other entrants a run for their money. Before beginning, she asked, "Which do you think is better, 'dropped to the floor' or 'fell to the floor'?" I said I would have to hear the whole thing before trying to answer that.

Sagi stood there, tall in the doorway between my room and the upstairs hall, and began:

> "There once was a woman named Helen,
>
> who fell when she slipped on a melon.
>
> She dropped to the floor,
>
> slid out the door,
>
> and where she is now there's no tellin'. "

It was good. I stood up and said, "Sagi, you've won." She looked at me. "Yes," she said, "I know."

# Rose Fitzgerald Kennedy

Written November 22, 2008

We were sharing a cottage with friends on the south shore of Cape Cod in the late 1970s when someone suggested visiting Nantucket. The next day we drove over to Hyannis, boarded the ferry, and departed for the island of scrimshaw.

As we passed the Kennedy houses, Sagi asked, "What was it like when John F. Kennedy was president?"

"The world was different then," I answered.

"How was it different?" she wanted to know.

"I was young and in the army, stationed at Fort Holabird," I said, "on Chesapeake Bay, not far from Washington, D.C., where Jonathan lived."

"Is he the army buddy who liked coffee ice cream?" she asked.

"Yes, he is," I said. "From some upstairs windows in his family's house one could see the National Cathedral. When Jonathan was a boy, he sang in a choir there. Later, to earn money for college, he worked at what passed for a White Castle restaurant in Georgetown. JFK was a senator from Massachusetts at that time. He and his wife, Jackie, lived in Georgetown. Thursday was their cook's night off, and Jackie sometimes went to White Castle to buy hamburgers for her husband's dinner. Rumor had it that Jack liked them. Knowing things like that made Jonathan, for me, a Washington insider. In those days, everyone wanted to be 'cool.' I thought Jonathan was the coolest of them all. He trimmed his sideburns at an angle, just as the Kennedy brothers did. We all followed his lead, in the hope that a little of his 'cool' would rub off on us."

* * * * * * *

Almost thirty years have passed since Sagi and I crossed Nantucket Sound together. I am now the same age Rose Kennedy was when she danced with her son at his inauguration ball. She would be 118 years old if she were alive today, but it seems like yesterday that she was telling photographers, "No close-ups, please, just soft lens, please."

The Kennedy years were invigorating. I don't think it ever occurred to any of us that they would end so soon and so sadly.

On weekends we took the train to New York City, always hoping that Maria Callas would be back at the Metropolitan Opera, but for that to happen, we had to wait until *Tosca* in 1965. When Pablo Casals played the cello at the Kennedy White House in November,

1961, we were beginning a year of duty at Army Language School in Monterey, California. Life was good. The country was younger then, and full of hope. By some miracle, something of the hope that suffused the national atmosphere back then has returned to grace us now. In spite of grievous blows to the nation's psyche – assassinations, wars, an attempted assassination, AIDS, and financial collapse – hope is back in the national conversation.

After almost fifty years, we are finding that we have not lost the ability to hope. What we have perhaps lost is the fear of hoping. I think we've been afraid to hope because the odds against it seemed so overwhelming. As a result, hope went into hiding.

We need to remember that hope is not something that is guaranteed by a document gathering dust in a drawer somewhere. Hope is a gift that has to be energetically endorsed and celebrated by those who lead us. It has to be exchanged within the body politic on a daily basis. It has been said that when their leaders lack vision, the people perish. Hope is like that vision; without it, the spirit can be extinguished. Nations need leaders who are willing to put aside private preferences in order to work for the public good. May that be their vision and our hope.

# Piper-Heidsieck

It was well after four o'clock in the afternoon when we arrived by car in Reims. On the right-hand side of the highway we saw the big buildings where thousands of bottles of champagne are stored in huge cellars. Large signs on the lawns proclaimed the names of some of the most celebrated champagnes in the world.

Hoping to take a tour of one of these famous places, we stopped first at one, then at a second and a third, but the answer was always the same: "So sorry, we are closing now; the last tour left fifteen minutes ago." I returned to the car, and we went on to the next: Piper-Heidsieck.

Without much spring left in my step, I walked toward the entrance. As I approached, the glass doors opened. Two young people, Monique and Théo, smartly dressed and smiling, introduced themselves and welcomed me to Piper-Heidsieck. I thanked them.

Monique asked, "What can we do for you today?"

By now my request was well-rehearsed: "We crossed the Atlantic from the United States this morning and drove here from Luxembourg this afternoon." I turned toward the car. Sagi waved. "We have to be in Paris tomorrow morning. Is there any chance of touring your facility this afternoon?"

The two of them waved back to Sagi, and without a moment's hesitation, Théo said, "But of course, sir, certainly. We understand. We are, in fact, closed, but we would consider it a pleasure to make an exception for you, our friends from America. Come in, Piper-Heidsieck at your service. Follow us, right this way, please."

\* \* \* \* \* \* \*

Our hosts were gracious. They made it seem as if they had all the time in the world for us.

An electric cart appeared. We seated ourselves in it, and the tour began. We passed through one long corridor after another, all of them filled with bottles in racks that reached almost to the vaulted ceiling. Along the way there were several stops for short films and recorded information. Once we got out of the cart to observe how bottles are rotated. We saw how quickly it can be done, then tried it for ourselves.

Monique told us the company was founded by Florens-Louis Heidsieck in the 1780s. While the Marquis de Lafayette helped George Washington and his troops win the Revolutionary War, Monsieur Heidsieck established Heidsieck Champagne in France.

His grandnephew, Charles-Camille Heidsieck, introduced champagne to America in the decade before the Civil War. In New York City they called him Champagne Charlie, but he lost everything after the

*130*

war began and ended up in prison.

He appealed to President Abraham Lincoln and was released. A friend gave him some old deeds to land in Denver, which was now a thriving city. Heidsieck sold the land and was able to start over.

Théo concluded, "Fifty years later, the First World War broke out here in Europe. Reims, its cathedral, and the surrounding countryside were made a wasteland. The Americans came to help in the war effort. A generation later they returned to help again. The U.S.-French connection goes back a long way, to the very beginnings of the American republic. We are grateful to America. We will never forget what you have done for us. France and Piper-Heidsieck appreciate and value their American friends. We have welcomed large numbers of Americans* for a long time."

The tour was over. Glasses of Piper-Heidsieck Rosé NV were waiting for us. We thanked our hosts.

"It was a pleasure," they said. "We thank you for visiting Piper-Heidsieck today."

---

* No official records are kept, but in 2008 the American Embassy in Paris estimated that more than 100,000 U.S. citizens reside in France.

# The Marne

We stopped to see the smiling angel at Reims Cathedral. "I wonder why he's smiling," I said.

"Maybe he's just had a surreptitious sip of champagne," Sagi suggested. She was seventeen.

It had been a long day, and it wasn't over yet. Our hotel was next to a soccer stadium. There was a sold-out game that evening, so we packed a picnic supper and drove south, through the vineyards that are the heart of the champagne country, to see the statue of Dom Pérignon in Épernay. "They should add one of the Veuve Clicquot," said Sagi. "There's plenty of room."

Shortly after that, we saw the Marne River for the first time. The mood turned pensive. Paris lay seventy miles to the west. Tomorrow we would visit Château-Thierry, site of some of the fiercest fighting of World War I, and then, twenty-five miles from Paris, we would see the Marne again. Perhaps because the river looms so large in history, Sagi expressed surprise at how ordinary-looking it was. Her comment reminded me of Hannah Arendt's use of the word "banal" in connection with the Adolf Eichmann trial in Jerusalem during the early 1960s.

My grandmother's youngest brother, Henry, fought in France during the First World War and was hospitalized for a long time in England. A generation later, his son was in uniform.

One day, while I helped my grandmother with some old trunks in the attic, she showed me a bound collection of maps – their pages worn and falling apart – that she had used to locate the battlefields where her brother had been. There was also a stereoscope with a box of photographs taken in war-ravaged France when the fighting was over. She looked at them for a while, and then, with a sigh, she gave them to me. I saw the stacked dead, the destruction, and the despair in the eyes of those who survived.

Now, with Sagi, I tried to comprehend that thousands had died within a few miles of where we were standing. The fact is staggering. The mind recoils from focusing on the grim horror of it. The enormity of what happened there was beyond my understanding. I closed my eyes and turned away, just as I had turned away from looking at the sepia-tinted stereoscopic pictures in the attic of my grandmother's house when I was a child.

I remember my friends, Brigitte and Marcel-Paul Guégnaud, owners of the Moulin Garnier near Tours, telling me that Marcel's parents had never taken him to visit Verdun because they could not bear the thought of it.

For the French, the First World War, what they call the "Great War," is the defining moment of the twentieth century. All across the country every year on November 11, the French gather at monuments in their cities, towns, and villages to remember those who died in a war that left many families with neither fathers nor sons.

Both Reims and Épernay were occupied cities when the Miracle of the Marne occurred. Hundreds of Paris taxicabs were requisitioned and used to transport thousands of troops to the Marne. In the ensuing battle, the enemy turned and ran.

The next day we arrived in Paris. We drove along the Seine until we saw the Cathedral of Notre Dame up ahead. Our hotel was just a few minutes away. We could see the new multi-purpose arena at Bercy, but it was too far away for us to hear what was happening there.

Eiffel Tower, Paris

# The Eiffel Tower

The Paris Exhibition took place in 1889, one hundred years after the French Revolution. Gustave Eiffel's structure for it was chosen from a competition that included a hundred designs. At the time of its construction, the three-hundred-meter tower was called the tallest building in the world. It has three platforms, including the one at the top. The tower is most often pictured from the Trocadero, which is northwest across the Seine River. It is sometimes said to be the most famous landmark on the planet.

The City of Paris is divided into twenty arrondissements. The seventh, where the Eiffel Tower is located, has the shape of an open fan, including a notch at the bottom for the thumb. The park for the tower, the Champ-de-Mars, forms a long rectangle on the left side of the fan.

During our visit we bought artisanal bread at Le Nôtre – near the École Militaire – and had a picnic in the Japanese Garden that is part of the UNESCO compound not far away. We visited the American Library and shopped at the market in the rue Cler. There are many small streets in the neighborhood, and one can find handsome buildings along all of them.  A walk down the block is a pleasant experience for those who live, work, and visit here.

After dinner on our first night in Paris, while walking back to our hotel, we rounded a corner and, looking up, saw the Eiffel Tower looming over us, so large it reminded us of King Kong in New York City in the 1933 movie.  One doesn't realize how immense the tower is until it is seen from the quiet streets nearby.

The night before we left for Switzerland, we decided to have dinner in the restaurant on the first platform of the tower.  The tables were not as close to one another as they sometimes are in French restaurants, but they were close enough for diners to overhear conversations at other tables.  I'm sure people listened in on us as the evening wore on because the arrival of salad plates at our table marked the beginning of a long and intense conversation that must have confirmed in the minds of those sitting near us that everything the French say about Americans being an odd lot is true.

I took one look at my plate and said, "I would like to take this home with me."  That one sentence, so simple and innocuous as far as I was concerned, triggered an immediate, avalanche-like response that started out with "Don't even think about it."

It was the kind of white plate one finds in restaurants all over France, except that this one had a thin green line around the rim.  This line had a break in it that left an empty space about as wide as my thumb; in that opening there was a graceful outline, also in green, of the Eiffel Tower.  I found it charming.

"People take things from restaurants all the time," I said. "Remember the Hofbräuhaus? It's expected, and besides, it's good advertising. The restaurants cover these losses by charging higher prices." I didn't really believe this, but I'd heard it said so often that I decided, more for the sake of argument than anything else, to try it. No luck.

"It's what is commonly referred to as stealing," came the anticipated and not-all-that-surprising response.

In spite of having spent a good deal of time in a great many souvenir shops in Paris, this plate was the only thing I liked, and I said so, again, repeating myself.

Sagi was mortified. Continuing this topic of conversation, in her opinion, went far beyond inane. She called it "carrying on." "A father of mine," she said, "here in Paris, of all places, wanting to steal a plate, and one with a little green tower on it at that." I could see I was asking too much.

I decided to recast the request. I proposed instead that we ask the waiter if it might be possible to buy several of the little plates. I thought the idea of one for each of us might mollify Sagi and work in my favor, but this suggestion was met with even stiffer resistance. The avalanche, already thundering down, now threatened to bury me alive, for if there is one thing worse than a father caught in the act of stealing, it is a father who says something to embarrass his child. Pure scorn, well-laced with caustic comments, fell upon me. This latest effort on my part was met with, maybe not horror exactly, but certainly by the release of an amount of opprobrium so great that I began to wonder if I had raised a child who might prefer seeing her father arrested and taken away without further ado to one of those dank dungeons that can still, no doubt, be found in the city of Paris today. And, by the way, wasn't one of them located just across the river from where we were sitting at that very moment, not far from the Place de la what's-its-name, where the guillotine had done its grisly work? Anything, from Sagi's point of view, was probably better than being party to the spectacle (for spectacle it would surely be) of her father begging for a plate with a green tower on it.

To make a long story a little shorter, I accepted defeat. There was no way I would be able to prevail in this matter, so I resigned myself to going away without a plate of remembrance. However, as everyone knows, remnants of childish intransigence survive in all of us and maybe in some of us more than in others.

"Yes," said Sagi, years later, "and those remnants seem to have been especially strong in one 'adult' American male of my acquaintance whose daughter did not allow him to have his own way with a small plate while his family was on vacation in a large European city that shall remain nameless."

I knew before leaving the restaurant that I would remember this evening for the rest of my life. As you can see, I have made a start.

\* \* \* \* \* \* \*

As the years pass, I regret having made it my odious practice to mention the beautiful little plate, how I lost it and whose fault that was, at every opportunity, opportune and inopportune alike. I did not discriminate. That plate, like the cat that could not be gotten rid of, just kept coming back.

I wrote a letter, in French that wasn't very good, but which I hoped would win some sympathy by virtue of its being so obviously heartfelt, to the restaurant and asked about the plate. After what seemed an unconscionably long time to keep me waiting – a small eternity even – someone was kind enough to write back in beautiful French to say the restaurant no longer had any of those plates. The writer said they were *anciennes*, which I took to mean old, thrown out, and replaced by something I knew could never be as attractive as the plate I had fallen in love with at first sight. The letter closed by saying I might be able to find one somewhere in a junk shop.

That day has not yet arrived, despite my best efforts to make it happen. Every year when I return from what are now, since my retirement, annual pilgrimages to France, or what Sagi has taken to calling "Quests for the holy plate," my friends ask me, "Well, did you find the plate this time?" And every year I have to tell them, "No, I haven't found it yet."

One holiday, a few years ago, Sagi said to me, "Daddy, I

should have helped you with that plate. I'm sorry I didn't." Those words comforted me a little, and it may be that I no longer think about the plate as often as I once did, but even so, sometimes when I'm in France, I still look for it.

# Paris Blue

Lynn Saint James transferred from Augustana College to Boston University at the end of her sophomore year. We lost touch with each other.

A few years later I was in Stuttgart, in what was then West Germany, with hometown friends who were visiting relatives there. Germany's first television tower had been built in Stuttgart, and on the last night of my stay, we had dinner in its restaurant. At eleven o'clock that evening, I boarded the Orient Express for Paris. I arrived at the Gare de l'Est early the next morning.

I checked my suitcase at American Express, took my overnight bag, and walked south across the city, past the Cathedral of Notre Dame, all the way to the Cité Universitaire, where I had booked a room a few weeks earlier.

That evening, while reading the *International Herald Tribune* in the campus center library, I looked up and saw Lynn Saint James sitting across the table from me.

"John," she exclaimed, "is it really you?"

"Yes, Lynn, it is," I answered. "What are you doing here in

France?"

"I majored in French," she replied. "I've been living in Aix, and I'm staying here at the Cité this summer while my apartment is being renovated."

For the next several days, Lynn showed me the city and introduced me to her friends. One night we were invited to dinner in Montmartre. The apartment was on the fourth floor. From its living room windows, one could look out across the rooftops of Paris and see the Eiffel Tower in the distance.

While Lynn and the others prepared dinner, I listened to Bartók's Concertos for Piano* and Orchestra and marveled at the view. Paris is closer to the North Pole than to the Equator, and there is something magical about the light of its long summer evenings. As I watched, the color of the sky slowly changed until, finally, I asked Lynn to join me at the window.

She walked over, stood beside me for a moment, and said, "That's what they call Paris blue. Beautiful, isn't it?"

"Yes, " I said, "it really is." I never forgot that color.

As the years with Sagi passed, I told her about Paris blue. Sometimes I would say, "Look, that color reminds me of …," or "That's close to – something like – Paris blue."

Sagi, for her part, would now and again look at something and ask, "Is that what Paris blue is like?" and I would have to answer, "No, not quite."

* The pianist was Géza Anda of Hungary.

During Sagi's first visit to France, we looked for Paris blue, but it eluded us until the evening we took a boat trip on the Seine. We crossed the Avenue Montaigne to reach the quay. We were waiting to go on board when Sagi touched my arm and said, "Look at the sky, over there by the tower, is that Paris blue?"

I looked up, and then I said, "Yes, Sagi, that's it."

Orient Express

# Fontainebleau

I.    The Storm, 1960

As we drove north toward Paris that summer morning, we could see the storm gathering strength as it moved inland from the Atlantic.

By nine o'clock it was increasingly apparent that our hopes for staying ahead of the threatening weather were almost certainly doomed. Darkness was fast overtaking us. The clouds were massing directly overhead, intimidating, like a gang of bullies that had orders from its ringleader to "take us out."

The sky turned as black as proverbial pitch. After that it looked like a giant oil slick, sliced through by smeary, writhing streaks of surreal color in unnerving shades of brutal blue and dirty purple laced with eerie, leaden gray. Only a painter like El Greco, or maybe Goya, could have imagined such colors, and used them.

The clouds looked as if they were boiling in an unseen, enormous cauldron. Then, bubbling over, they tumbled out and moved, in fits and starts, downward toward the ground.

This infernal scene was punctuated and made more ominous by thunder claps and slashing lightning strikes that were as vertical as exclamation marks. It was as though a thousand specters were readying themselves to bear witness to the end of time.

Orléans was behind us; halfway to Orly, it was becoming obvious as the minutes crept by that we weren't going to make it. In a little while the wind's full force would be loosed upon us. We had to think of something fast.

At the first opportunity, the car skittered off the main road, and we saw a small sign that read "Fontainebleau, 1.2 kilometers." We came to the Hôtel de Londres, which sits across and up the slope from the château. No sooner had we stopped than the storm broke upon us with all its wrath and fury. The three of us bolted from the car and ran for the terrace. The clouds opened, and the deluge began. It was a downpour for the history books. The utter drenching continued until the château courtyard across the street resembled a small smaragdine sea. Then the sky lightened a little, the rain slacked off a bit, and the clouds took on the shade of green one sees entombed in the ice in those parts of the world where the big white polar bears live.

That was when the hail began. Cowering under awnings and umbrellas, water splashing to our knees, we turned, looked toward the chateau and were astonished to see, as the hail continued, hundreds, more likely thousands, of hailstones about the size of ping pong balls falling upon the adjacent streets and then bouncing up again, three, four feet in the air, looking for all the world as if they were engaged in the most exuberant dance that France or any other place had ever seen, performed live.

It was an incredible, unforgettable sight that remains as vivid in my mind today as it was when I saw it happening as a young man just out of college, traveling in Europe for the first time. Never did I imagine that on my next visit to Fontainebleau I would be accompanied by a teen-age girl, and that she would be my daughter.

Hailstones

II.    The Horseshoe Staircase, 1983

I visited Fontainebleau for the first time almost fifty years ago. (I'm writing this in 2008.) It has been twenty-five years since Sagi and I were there. On the first visit, two friends and I arrived at Fontainebleau by chance, but the trip with Sagi was the result of thoughtful preparation. This time there was no storm; on the contrary, the weather was beautiful – cool and mild – almost autumnal.

It was Sagi's first trip to France, promised her by a proud parent as a reward for many years of studying French. She was a history buff, eager to see Fontainebleau and its horseshoe staircase from which, in 1814, Napoléon bade his troops farewell before going into exile on the island of Elba, not far from Corsica, where he was born.

Sagi and I had driven down from Paris. We parked the rented car near the spot where – almost a quarter century earlier – my friends and I had left our Peugeot. Back then, because of the storm's torrential rain, we had run from the car as if the devil himself had been right behind us. Today we got out, stretched our legs, and began our tour with the avenue of trees. Later on, we went inside the château.

Joséphine and Napoléon shared the happiest days of their lives here. It was gratifying to see how much remained from the time when they lived in these apartments. Something of their spirit survived. One could imagine the two of them walking in from the

*151*

next room. It was an extraordinary place. We were grateful to France for its being there and for sharing it with us.

We located the room, not the largest, where Napoléon had signed the abdication papers. From there we went outside again and found ourselves at the top of the storied staircase. This was what we had come to see. We waited for a while, hoping we might be able to build a memory to take away with us, instead of forgetting what we had seen as soon as we went out the gate, found the highway, and started back to Paris.

"I've always wanted to visit Fontainebleau," said Sagi, "and I am not disappointed in it, are you?"

"No, Sagi, I'm not," I answered. "It's the kind of place that brings one closer to history. There is an immediacy about it that one doesn't often find at historical sites."

"I wonder what it was like for him to stand here – what was going through his mind?" Sagi asked quietly.

"I guess we'll never know for certain what he was thinking," I answered, "but at least we can know we have been in the place where it happened."

Sagi said, "I wonder if he ever tried to think ahead, to cast himself forward in time, into the future, to try to imagine how it would be for people like us visiting here someday."

We were silent for a moment, feeling that the presence of the place was satisfaction enough. We began to move down the steps to our right, and then, as if responding to some unseen cue, we raced each other to the bottom, back up the other side and down again. Doing that, I think, is what has made the memory stick in our minds all these years.

"I can't imagine, can you, what it must be like for people who visit Fontainebleau without knowing what took place in this courtyard, the Cour des Adieux," Sagi said.

"No," I added, "I can't either."

"I'm going to major in history when I get to college," she added. "I'll probably have a second major, too, as you did, but I don't know yet what that will be."

When we reached the other side of the Cour des Adieux, we stopped and looked back at the staircase one last time. Then we returned to the car, got in, and drove away.

Horseshoe Staircase, Fontainebleau

# Tale of Two Lunches

It was California, and even though it seemed like a movie, it wasn't. We were just some U.S. Army guys driving around Sonoma County, north of San Francisco, on a weekend pass in the summer of 1962. We had come to Sonoma to see what was left of Jack London's house, but we ended up lost.

We found ourselves on a country road bordered by huge eucalyptus trees. Through the trees on the right there were fields; to the left there was forest. Up ahead, we saw a large stone building all covered with vines.

As we approached, the car's tires crunched the gravel in the courtyard. This was Buena Vista winery. It had been founded by a Hungarian count. That explained the raked gravel. We got out of the car, walked along the creek, and then toured the building. There was a quotation by Robert Louis Stevenson carved on an oak barrel, but I don't remember what it said.

\* \* \* \* \* \* \*

Fifteen years later, when I returned with Sagi, the barrel with the quotation was still there, but the courtyard had been covered with asphalt. The gravel was gone, and so was much of the magic.

To toast my army buddies, Sagi and I went back to town and bought a bottle of Buena Vista cabernet sauvignon. At an open market we found the makings for a French-style picnic: sausage, Delouis mustard, olives, Gruyère cheese, goat cheese, cucumbers, tomatoes, and a baguette. Back at the winery's picnic table, we prepared our small feast and opened the wine. It was velvet smooth in the throat and reminded me of dark berries, just as it had years before.

* * * * * * *

Sagi and I were in France in 1983. Early one morning, just as the sun was rising, we left Paris for Switzerland. We took the Autoroute southeast toward Dijon, hoping to reach Gevrey-Chambertin in time for lunch, but when we arrived, everything was closed for the afternoon. Having to go without lunch did not suit us, so we stopped at a restaurant and rapped on the window, even though the shade was drawn. A young woman opened the door and said, "We are closed, sorry," but then the chef appeared. He looked at us and said, "You are American, no?"

"Yes," I said, "we are."

"You are searching for lunch, right?"

"Yes," I said.

"No problem," he replied, "we are closed, but if you would like to come in and sit for a while, I will go into my kitchen and see what I can find to make you a fine American lunch, OK?"

"Yes," I said. "Thank you so much."

He showed us to a table, and we sat down. A little boy brought us napkins and French workingman's wine glasses. After some coaxing, his sister appeared and held out silverware for us. The chef returned, carrying a glass for himself and a bottle of Pouilly-Fuissé, 1958. He poured a little for himself, held the glass up to the light, tasted, then filled our glasses and said, "Welcome to Gevrey-Chambertin."

A few minutes later, he brought us our "American" lunch.

"Sandwiches, just like home, no?" he asked.

He continued, "I take everything American in my kitchen and make it for you. You like?" he asked.

"Yes," we said. "Very good."

It was the first time I had eaten a sandwich in more than twenty years.

When we finished our lunch, the chef walked us to the door, pointed across the street to a tasting room, and said, "They are open for you now." Then he asked, "Will we be seeing you for dinner this evening?"

"So sorry," I said, "but we are on the way to Pontarlier." Unbeknownst to us, the best dessert of the whole trip was waiting for us there.

# "To Thee Before the Close of Day"

The Cistercians are a contemplative monastic order. They were founded by reformist Benedictines in Burgundy, France, in the year 1098.

They were invited to Austria by Margrave Leopold III. Twelve monks and their abbot left the fields of France on the west side of the Alps and traveled east 500 miles, almost to the Hungarian plain, to the place that would become Heiligenkreuz (Holy Cross). They consecrated the monastery in 1133, thirty-five years after the founding of the order. Cistercian comes from the word "cistern," reminding us that they settled in the valleys, not on the hilltops. This was regarded as a mark of humility. Heiligenkreuz is surrounded by the Vienna woods.

The location contrasts sharply with those of the imposing abbeys of Melk and Göttweig, fifty miles to the northwest. Both of them overlook the Danube River and can be seen from far away. They present Catholicism at its grandest.

Heiligenkreuz is a different matter altogether. It is about understatement, not pomp and awe. In a still, small voice, it requests one's attention.  It does not shout.  It is dun colored.  For more than eight hundred years, it has cherished and devoted itself to music that is sung a cappella.

I remember when Sagi and I stopped at Heiligenkreuz the first time.  It was 1983.  The driver turned to us and said, "This is it." We looked around.

"Where is it?" I asked.  He pointed to a door in the nondescript courtyard wall that ran the length of the street.

"That's it?" I asked.

"That's it," he repeated.  "This is where people come to empty their minds, not to fill them."

When Sagi was a child, we concluded our days by singing "To Thee Before the Close of Day" ("*Te lucis ante terminum*") in a translation I found in an old Episcopal hymn book.  I liked the line "so calm our minds that fears may cease, and rested bodies wake in peace."  These words came back to me now.

Sagi crossed the street and tried the door.  It was open.  We went in and soon found ourselves in the midst of some of the finest Romanesque architecture in Austria.  At one end of the nave, three narrow windows with rounded tops and plain glass made for a study in quiet glory.

"Franz Schubert sometimes played the organ here," I said.

"But we haven't come to hear the organ, have we?" Sagi asked.

"No," I answered. "We've come to hear the monks chant the

same prayers that have been part of vespers here for eight hundred and fifty years."

Sagi and I found places near the choir stalls and waited for the service to begin. When it did, it was otherworldly, transcendent. Although we could see the monks sitting in their stalls, chanting, the sound seemed to emanate from the hallowed space itself rather than from those who chanted.

It was beautiful, and then, toward the end of the service, we heard the Latin words that we had come for: "*Te lucis ante terminum.*" It was like answered prayer. That's all there was, and that was all there needed to be.

\* \* \* \* \* \* \*

Now it is summer of 2008. Stift Heiligenkreuz is celebrating eight hundred and seventy-five years. The monks have made a recording that has brought attention to them and to Heiligenkreuz. In addition to the familiar dread of fire and flood, those who cultivate the inner life will have to deal with a world that could be too much with them.

Heiligenkreuz

*162*

# A Little More Time

"Sagi," I said, as she was passing through the dining room, "we received a letter from your calculus teacher today. He's concerned about your work in his class. Your last test wasn't so good. Has he spoken with you about this?"

"Yes," she answered softly, "he has."

Trying to adjust to her tone, I asked, "Do you have time just now to sit with me so we can talk about it?" She did not say yes or no, but stopped on the other side of the table, giving me a chance to continue. "I think he expects a response from me, and I don't know what to tell him. Can you help me?"

Sagi didn't say anything. Her manner was somewhere beyond subdued, almost wounded, but I knew the strength of her resolve. "Do you want to sit down?" I asked, trying for gentleness, but at the same time thinking I'm just a rough hugger-mugger kind of guy who tries to get it right, but more often than not, ends up falling short.

Sagi sat down and began telling me about the class. I tried to settle down, wanting to do my best for this child who had centered my life since the day she was born.

As I sat there, holding the letter from her teacher, it was almost impossible for me to keep my thoughts under control. Painful memories overwhelmed me. I wondered if Sagi was having the same problems I had encountered when I was her age. I was afraid she had somehow inherited whatever this was from me. I was shaken by a fear so palpable that I could hardly speak.

There were times when I did not hear what Sagi was saying. I had to ask her to repeat things. As she, ever patient, stayed with me, I realized that what she was describing had nothing in common with what I had found myself trapped in when I was a teenager. Sagi was able to do the work. Her problem was she never had enough time to finish all of it. My problem had been I did not know how to begin.

Relieved, I told her I would write a letter asking her teacher to make a distinction between those who, given a little more time, could complete the tests and those who, like myself, would never be able to solve the problems, not even if they were given all the time in the world.

"What do you think of that idea?" I asked.

"It's good," she said. "Thank you."

"I'll write the letter after dinner," I said. "You can look at it and tell me if there's anything that needs changing."

Later that evening I finished the letter. Sagi approved it and took it along to school the next morning. Her grades improved; we never heard from her teacher again.

\* \* \* \* \* \* \*

Looking back on it now, the answer we were seeking seems not that hard to find, yet, at that moment, for someone like me, who had such a difficult time with math – and whose life had changed because of it – this conversation between daughter and father was anything but simple. My experience with math years ago rose up, and it wasn't easy for me to focus as well as I wanted to on Sagi's situation.

My friends and I grew up enjoying amiable competition with one another: Eldon in the 100-yard dash, David on Minnesota's political science test. Grady and I were so well matched at the piano that when our teacher, Mrs. Shore, closed her eyes, she could not tell which one of us was playing.

But that all changed when it came to math. It was then that I began to fall seriously behind. Regardless of how hard I tried, or how much help was given, I could not do the work. I found myself in a bad patch, alone.

Almost forty years have passed since I first read John Bowlby's *The Growth of Love* (see earlier story, "One Hand Clapping"). There is still much to be learned about abstract reasoning powers and how they can be damaged. Those who have suffered such injury need help in coping with the problems that result, and everything possible should be done to prevent injury from occurring.

Rolls-Royce

# Penelope Keith

In the first program of the BBC comedy series *Good Neighbors*, the audience does not see Margot (played by Penelope Keith), but they do hear her speak. This happens at the end of the show. There is something so arresting about what she says and how she says it that expectation sits in the air until the second program is broadcast. It is worth waiting for because Margot, when seen for the first time, is everything one has never dreamed of finding in a British housewife.

In spite of her sometimes simpering good manners, one has a sense of being in the proximity of an explosion waiting to happen; it will be a genteel explosion, no doubt about that, but the release it brings will be second to none. It is clear from the beginning that Margot is a force of nature. She incarnates the "eternal feminine" that inspired Beethoven; she is what the world cannot live without. Trying to deal with her, her husband Jerry (played by Paul Eddington) finds himself in a place that is way too deep for him. He has no more chance of coming out ahead of her than a snowball has of coming out of a very hot place. Lurking beneath Margot's silks and satins, there is something poised, ready to pounce: a purring power that would throw Attila into a panic of the first order.

In *Good Neighbors* she can be found driving a Volvo, and that's nice, but a woman like Margot needs a Rolls, and in the BBC's *To the Manor Born*, that is what she gets, but now she isn't Margot anymore. She has left the south suburbs of London and has landed in the English countryside as Audrey Forbes-Hamilton, owner of a venerable Rolls-Royce and not much else. She has found her destiny, and its name is Grantleigh. *To the Manor Born* is the story of what happens between her moving out of the big house on the Grantleigh estate and her moving back in again. It is a fairy tale for children of all ages.

Audrey is brisk, her hair is not long like Margot's, and she has traded loose-fitting togs for tailored tweeds. She has quickened her pace and lengthened her stride, but she has lost none of her formidable strength. She steps into the role of Audrey as if it were a second skin. We are delighted. Without a moment's hesitation, we fall in line behind her, charmed by the person she has become and ready to follow her over every hill and dale at Grantleigh.

For her we will sit up straight, keep our elbows at our sides, take small bites, and – lest her Wellingtons be sullied – throw our Eddie Bauer goose down jackets into the muckiest of mud holes without so much as a murmur. While doing all of this, we will not forget to pronounce "finance," "jewelry," and "diamond" correctly.

By any democratic measure, Audrey is way over the top, but

it's all right with us because she is the person we think of when we look at the posters in the town library that exhort us to be all that we can be. She is supremely confident. This is what we are all hoping to be. She is an ideal, someone to emulate, the master of all she surveys.

With Audrey in charge, no slip will be made between the cup and the lip. We can rest assured she will never forget to dot an "i" or cross a "t." What's more, she will fill in the blanks or have them deleted.

There are some who might say Audrey Forbes-Hamilton is a snob. I invite them to stand next to her on a theater stage that is equipped with an audience applause meter. They will quickly learn who it is the audience prefers. Deep down we know that if we should ever have occasion to change places with her, we would probably do the same things she does. Watching her is satisfying in a primal kind of way. She meets a need we all have to prevail over others. We would all be Audreys if we could manage it. To say we wouldn't is to join those unhappy souls who disparage what they cannot have. She not only has what it takes, she flaunts it, something many people are loath to do for themselves, but don't mind too much if others do it for them.

Audrey is the imperial foe we want to have on our side. When someone has only himself to blame for getting caught in her line of fire, we watch what comes next with unalloyed glee. One look at her in command mode and we know that someone, somewhere, is about to meet his Waterloo. It could be anyone, anywhere. Who knows, if she had been in the vicinity at the time of Henry VIII, one wife might have been enough.

She has a rich uncle. He invites her to lunch with him at his club in London. As uncle and niece pass through the dining room, they see two men – one of them possibly wearing a clip-on tie – seated at a small table. Audrey knows who they are by reputation and has good reason to dislike them. Her uncle introduces her. Both men remain seated. Audrey waits for a second, then she says, "Please, don't get up." On hearing this, they jump to their feet, but it's too late. She has nailed them. The moment is priceless, and it is not lost on her uncle. Grace, he knows, has value and prerogatives; it deserves to be enhanced by inheritance.

\* \* \* \* \* \* \*

Someone once gave Sagi two large stuffed panda bears. She named them Penelope and Keith and wrote a letter to Ms. Keith telling her about them. A few weeks later, a letter written on blue paper arrived from London. It was from Penelope Keith. In it she thanked Sagi for the letter and said she was pleased to know the pandas had been named Penelope and Keith.

# Mondale Rally, 1984

It was ten o'clock in the evening. Sagi had finished her calculus homework earlier than usual. I asked if she was interested in going downtown to see the finish of the "Mondale for President" rally. To my surprise, she said, "Let's go!" Usually she declared "lights out" as soon as her homework was done.

"Just think, this is the first time I'll be old enough to vote in a presidential election," she said, as we hurried out to the car.

Traffic was heavy as soon as we left the neighborhood. Cars were at a near standstill on Interstate 94, so we took side streets until we reached the monument commemorating the Grand Army of the Republic – east across the street from the Cathedral of St. Paul, south across the freeway from the Minnesota State Capitol.

The city of St. Paul sits on seven hills, as Rome does. We were on Cathedral Hill, with a good view of downtown. We couldn't go any farther for the moment; traffic was snarled for blocks around the intersection of I-94 and I-35E, so we stopped alongside the monument and waited.

St. Paul is home to both the state capitol, designed by Cass

Gilbert, a Minnesota native, and the Cathedral of St. Paul, planned by Emmanuel Louis Masqueray, a Frenchman. The domes of both buildings were illuminated and looking their impressive best. Half a mile apart, linked by Archbishop John Ireland Boulevard, the two landmarks complement each other. They are grand and as agreeably proportioned as anything one finds in Italy, although F. Scott Fitzgerald liked to say the cathedral reminded him of a bulldog sitting on its haunches.

The cathedral stone is gray. At night it seems more majestic and mysterious than the gleaming white marble of the state capitol. Archbishop Ireland, who had lived in France for seven years, invited the French architect to build the cathedral. Monsieur Masqueray arrived in St. Paul in 1905 and lived here until his death on May 26, 1917. Archbishop Ireland's health began to fail later that same year. He died September 25, 1918. The archbishop and the architect spoke French with each other and called the cathedral their child.

\* \* \* \* \* \* \*

As we waited for the traffic to abate, Sagi pointed in the direction of the Radisson Hotel and asked, "Doesn't that hotel have a revolving restaurant on its top floor?"

"Yes," I said, "it does. It used to be a Hilton, and now it's a Radisson."

"Do you remember the afternoon we went up there to have

apple pie and ice cream?" Sagi asked. "It was after I had a vaccination shot at Dr. Steinberg's office. Amazing. That's more than a dozen years ago."

She was right. What we could not know at the time was that more than *two* dozen years would pass before we would go up there again, and that when the day came for us to re-visit the restaurant, we would find ourselves in the company of a little girl still celebrating her third birthday. Sophie, Sagi's daughter, looked out the big windows on the twenty-second floor and said, "There's a train moving on railroad tracks down there, next to the river."

Sophie has red hair, the same color as a few errant red hairs that have been hiding in my eyebrows for years and only showed themselves when they failed to turn gray at the same time as the rest of me.

The traffic cleared, but we talked for a while longer and then drove down to the auditorium, hoping to catch a glimpse of the Mondales and Ms. Ferraro – or their vehicles   as they left the rally.

When we reached Kellogg Boulevard, a policeman told us the rally was over. The principals had gone home for the night, so we left, too. We hadn't seen anyone famous, but we had been close to history being made.

Sagi said, "This will open more doors for women. Little by little, we'll get there."

She was right. Sandra Day O'Connor had been serving on the Supreme Court since 1981. Ruth Bader Ginsburg would join the court in 1993. It was only a matter of time until other women would take their rightful places.

# The P-Word

Evelyn lived in a building so big that semitrailer trucks could pass right through it. After they drove inside, they stopped on a scale to be weighed. There was a long window between the passage where the scale was and the office where Evelyn wrote down the results. When she finished, she took the papers out and handed them to the drivers. Often she was in a hurry, forgetting to close the door between the office, which was part of her family's living quarters, and the passage, which was open to the breezes that came in off the Mississippi River half a block away. In warm weather the cool air was welcome, but when the weather was cold, no one liked it.

Evelyn's sister, Ardee, my elementary school teacher, and Ardee's husband, Vic, always spent the winter holidays with Evelyn and her family. Listening to the sisters talk was like being in a front row seat at a Broadway show. When Evelyn forgot to close the door, Ardee would call out, "Hey, what's the matter with you? Were you born in a barn?" Evelyn would reply, loudly enough for all to hear, "Yes, I was, and every time I hear an ass bray, it makes me homesick."

I knew from church that Evelyn's word for donkey was in the Bible, so I guessed it was all right for her to say it, but I was just a boy and thought it best not to try it myself.

* * * * * * *

In October, 1962, I was driving back to Minnesota after a year spent studying Russian at Army Language School in Monterey, California. It was the time of the Cuban missile crisis, and I was listening to the car radio. Near the summit of Rabbit Pass in Colorado, I heard President Kennedy's ambassador to the United Nations, Adlai Stevenson, address a question about missiles in Cuba to the Soviet Union's representative. When there was no response, Mr. Stevenson paused for a moment before saying, in a stern voice that I had never heard him use before, "Well, sir, I am prepared to wait for your answer until hell freezes over." Hearing that from the mild-mannered, well-spoken Mr. Stevenson worked like a stun gun on his audience. It was followed by complete and utter silence.

"That's what one might call an example of righteous indignation," I thought. I hoped my soldier life as an interpreter-interrogator would not place me in many situations like that, but if it did, at least I knew how to tell interrogees where to get off.

* * * * * * *

The years went by, and I do not recall ever having been surprised by any particular word spoken at our dining room table, but then one evening Sagi came in, sat down, and began telling about an unfortunate incident that had taken place that afternoon at track and field practice. As the story continued, I thought, "Wow, what happened out there would be enough to make a preacher swear," but I was not prepared for what came next. Sagi concluded by saying, "Boy, was coach _ _ _ _ _ _!"

My head continued making the movements an earnest listener makes, but my mind veered off track, no pun intended. I didn't look up, react, or respond in any visible way. I did think of saying, "What! A child of mine, using a word like that, and right here at the dinner table," but I let it pass. After all, I was forty-four years old. I had learned there are times when it is better to remain silent and be thought old-fashioned than it is to open one's mouth and remove all doubt.

## *Elephants Can Remember*

Why do people send their children away to school? I asked myself this question a dozen times a day when Sagi began thinking about choosing a college. On the one hand, I wanted her to have a great adventure. On the other, I wondered what would happen to the conversation the two of us had carried on for eighteen years. The more important thing, I decided, was the adventure.

One doesn't see parent birds helping their little ones down the trunk of the tree, settling them comfortably on the ground below, and saying, "There now, go, have an adventure." No, what one sees is little birds bumbling out of the nest and then, God willing, flying.

When the college catalogs began arriving, I organized them alphabetically in a file box I found in the basement. Later on, as the flood of catalogs continued, I divided them into four groups: Minnesota, Midwest, East Coast, and West Coast. It wasn't long before I noticed the East Coast was getting most of the attention. Now and then I put in a good word for a college in Minnesota, or one in the Upper Midwest, but I knew the decision would not be mine to make.

Sagi chose Bryn Mawr, a college in Pennsylvania with Quaker roots. We bought a trunk; she packed it full and sent it on ahead. Then we waited for her departure date. It came. She took a small bag, as if she were flying off for the weekend, but I knew she was going away forever, and everything would change. Her cherished daily presence in my life had come to an end.

I missed her so much, I found a second job – this one at a downtown bank – that took me from four in the afternoon until midnight. Sometimes I drove to the park across the Mississippi River Gorge from the airport and watched the planes flying in and out. On weekends I went out to the Lindbergh Terminal McDonald's and wrote my weekly letter at the table where we had often eaten French fries together.

At first she wrote long letters every day, trying to keep me in the loop, but, little by little, college life took more and more of her time. The letters became fewer, and they were shorter. I tried to hold her in my mind. I tried to keep the time we'd had together alive. In the hope of finding an Agatha Christie mystery, I went to the local library. I didn't really care for mysteries, but it was one way to keep my memory from fading. There was just one Christie book on the shelf: *Elephants Can Remember*. I checked it out and took my time reading. When I finished, I noted it on a list of topics to talk about during the holidays.

When Sagi came home, I told her I had read an Agatha Christie mystery.

"Good," she said. "How did you like it?"

"Oh, I don't know," I answered, "not bad, OK, I guess."

"Which one was it?" she asked.

"*Elephants Can Remember*," I answered.

"Oh, Daddy," she said softly, and her voice was kind. "You're hopeless. Agatha Christie said that was the worst book she ever wrote."

# New Jersey Turnpike

Sagi had some free time, so we rented a car and drove from Philadelphia to New York City to look at some paintings in the Metropolitan Museum of Art. Even though it was out of the way, we took the George Washington Bridge into the city because it was the route I knew best. Taking FDR Drive south along the East River brought us to the Upper East Side; we drove west across Manhattan until the museum came into view. Luck was on our side. Two blocks from Fifth Avenue, there was a vacant parking space.

The first painting on our list was Johannes Vermeer's *Young Woman with a Jug*. Because of its straight sides, the jug had always looked more like a pitcher to us, but we knew that was a matter of debate among art historians. When we finished looking at the painting, it was time for lunch. There used to be a restaurant to the left as one entered the museum, and we went to look for it. The waiter declared the salmon and cucumber salad a "good choice," and it arrived promptly. After lunch we looked at paintings by Guy Péne du Bois and Edward Hopper before going to the American Wing to see a Minnesota living room.

A Frank Lloyd Wright house in Deephaven, Minnesota, was torn down in the 1970s, but its living room was saved from demolition and taken to the Metropolitan. It was a strange sensation, standing in a living room that had once been part of a house on a Minnesota road we knew well. After visiting the museum gift shop and buying some postcards of the Vermeer painting, we returned to the car and left for Pennsylvania.

We hadn't had any problems finding our way from Bryn Mawr to the New Jersey Turnpike that morning. There were signs for both the turnpike and New York City, but now, driving in the opposite direction, it was a different story. After stopping in Princeton for coffee, we began looking for directions to Philadelphia, but there were none to be seen. We were reluctant to leave the turnpike, fearing it might be difficult to get back to it. Exits were not always paired with entrance ramps. I remembered John McPhee's piece in *The New Yorker* about the pine barrens in southern New Jersey, and I imagined them off to our left somewhere. Not wanting to risk ending up in the barrens with night coming on, we stayed on the turnpike until it ended, finally, at the Delaware border. I asked the attendant at the toll booth why there had not been any signs for Philadelphia, or Pennsylvania. He gave the impression of not understanding the question, but I think he'd heard it before.

Sagi and I went on to Bryn Mawr College and said our good-byes. I took the car downtown and caught a train for Washington, D.C., arriving in time to enjoy a late evening dinner with friends.

*184*

While waiting in line at National Airport early the next morning, I turned and found myself facing a businesswoman whose picture I remembered having seen on the cover of a Minnesota magazine. "Barbara," I said and almost immediately corrected myself.

"No need to apologize," she said. "People make that mistake all the time."

It was seven o'clock in the morning. Here she was, traveling alone, carrying her own suitcase.

"She probably has more than one jet of her own," I thought, "but she's taking the same plane I am, standing in line, waiting her turn."

She asked for my name. I thanked her for her support of Philip Brunelle and the Plymouth Music Series. She was gracious. I was grateful.

Soon after my return to Minnesota, Sagi called. "Guess what," she said, "I asked some friends here at school why we did not see a sign for Philadelphia when we were on the New Jersey Turnpike. Do you know what they said?"

"No," I replied, "I have no idea."

"They all laughed and said there are no signs because everybody knows the way to Philadelphia."

"Don't you realize there are people driving on the turnpike who are not from this part of the country?" Sagi had asked. "How are they supposed to know that?"

"Yes," said a friend of Sagi's from California. "It seems to me some Easterners forget that these roads are used by people from all fifty states and Canada, not to mention Europe and the rest of the world. They seem to forget there is more to this country than just the original thirteen colonies. There ought to be a sign for Philadelphia."

My sentiments exactly.

# Physics

I received my first wrist watch years ago when watches had to be wound. It was a Hamilton. Dad told me it's best to wind one's watch at the same time every day. He wound his watch at seven in the morning. I decided to do the same.

"Be careful not to wind it too much, or too little," he said, while showing me how to do it. There were white tulips blooming in the garden.

I followed his advice, but by the time school started, the watch had stopped running.

"No matter," Dad said, "we'll get you a new one for Christmas."

Christmas came and so did a new watch, an Elgin this time. Once again, my father explained. I paid careful attention, but was apprehensive. After a few weeks, this watch, too, stopped working. I didn't tell anybody, but eventually Dad found out. When he did, he said, "Your birthday is coming up soon. We'll get you another one."

My birthday arrived, bringing with it a Bulova watch. We went through the winding procedure again.

Until I left for college, a new wrist watch was almost always among my birthday and Christmas gifts. No one seemed to mind that I was wearing out a lot of watches.

Once or twice we took a watch to the local jeweler and asked if it could be repaired; if I remember correctly, these efforts were never successful. I always came home with a new watch.

After I went away to school, no one in my family ever mentioned wrist watches to me again. By the time I was in the army, I had stopped wearing a watch altogether and have not worn one since.

* * * * * * *

When Sagi started running with her school's track team, she asked for a wrist watch. I ordered one from the Orvis catalog. They had a "Satisfaction Guaranteed or your Money Back" policy. I thought that might be a good idea, just in case.

The watch arrived in time for Sagi's birthday in late summer, just before track practice started. I told her what my father had told me about winding a watch. After a few weeks, I noticed she was not wearing the watch. I asked her about it. She said it had stopped.

"No matter," I heard myself say, "we'll get you a new one for Christmas."

By the time track practice started in the spring, Sagi was no longer wearing the new watch. We said no more about watches.

Sagi began college with a major in history, just as I had done; later on, she added a second major, this one in physics, something I

*188*

had not done.  One day when she was a senior assisting other physics students, she telephoned and said, "I know why it is that neither of us can keep a watch running."  I was surprised.

"Why is that?" I asked.

"It's because approximately eight percent of the population has a magnetic field that interferes with the mechanism in a wind-up wrist watch."

"That's interesting," I said.

I think both of us were relieved to learn that our watches had stopped because of something over which we had no control.

* * * * * * *

One morning a few years ago I was having breakfast at Perkins with friends.  I told them about the problems Sagi and I have had with wind-up wrist watches.  I was taken aback when most people at the table expressed skepticism.  After breakfast I drove to Moeller's, a jewelry store in the Highland Park neighborhood of St. Paul, and asked to speak with a watchmaker.

He emerged from his little room, took off his thick glasses, and I asked my question.  He said he had heard that a person's magnetic field could interfere with the workings of a wrist watch, and then he added that he had even heard of a case where a man's magnetic field was so strong that his watch ran backwards.  At that point, I decided to let the matter rest.

J. Elsing

Tulips and Vegetable Garden

# Katharine Hepburn

Katharine Hepburn went to Bryn Mawr. Her dorm room was small, but it had a sixteen-foot balcony. Soon after Sagi started college, she wrote to tell us about that room. She said she hoped to live in it someday.

"If that day ever comes," she added, "it will most likely be during my senior year. Rooms are assigned by lottery. Senior women have first choice. Almost everyone wants to live in Katharine Hepburn's room, so keep your fingers crossed."

For the next three years, we kept it in mind.

The autumn of Sagi's senior year arrived. She had a good number, not a sure thing, but there was reason to hope. If the first name drawn did not take the room, Sagi thought she might get it, and that's what happened.

She moved in for her senior year. In October, I suggested she write to Ms. Hepburn to tell her how happy she was to be living in the room with the sixteen-foot balcony.

Being a Katharine Hepburn fan myself, I was pleased for Sagi's sake, but I knew it would probably be a while before she would have time to act on my suggestion.  She had a demanding schedule.

By this time in my life the words "Old, I hoped I would be wise, now I know I'm not" fit me quite well.  I decided to write to Ms. Hepburn myself.  She wrote back saying she was delighted to know my daughter was living in the room with the long balcony. She wondered where all the time had gone since she had lived there herself, then closed by saying she would never get anything done if she took time to answer all the letters people sent her and signed it "Katharine Hepburn."  I had the letter framed.

The following spring, Sagi wrote to Ms. Hepburn to tell her about the year she'd had in the room with the balcony.  Ms. Hepburn answered that letter, too.  It was apparent that writing was an effort for her.  This time she signed herself "K. Hepburn," thereby reducing by half the number of letters she needed to make her signature.

# The Funeral

Sagi's flight was delayed. Instead of coming in at eleven in the morning, it was now scheduled to arrive at half past noon. There was nothing to be done about it. I could only sit and wait; an hour and a half was too long a time to stand.

Somehow I was not surprised that "late" was going to play a part in the day. Actually, I think I had expected something like this to happen.

My adopted sister, Sagi's Aunt Marie, was born more than two months too soon, and this caused some health problems later in her life. Among other things, her liver and kidneys were weak.

I've sometimes wondered if her premature birth had anything to do with the way her life unfolded. As the years went by, it became apparent that she had a propensity for being late. I began to regard it as something like a congenital defect. Having been untimely born, it was as if she had, at some point, sworn a solemn oath declaring that she would never again be early for anything.

There was nothing for which she could not be late. In some ways being late defined who she was. She had a gift for making people wait, and after she became the church organist, some of those who had to wait for her were in coffins.

She took lateness to a whole new level. People adjusted to it: family, friends, neighbors, school bus drivers, teachers, classmates, members of the community, school principals, colleagues, pupils, and a church congregation.

She was a teacher for more than twenty years, but I don't think she ever arrived at school in time to hear the eight o'clock bell. After threatening to have her fired, a school principal told a neighbor of ours that if the Quakers had preachers, and if those preachers had to deal with my sister, it would drive all of them to drink.

Marie was known, however, not only for being late, but also for being kind, especially for staying after school to work with those who needed additional help, even if it made her late for dinner.

Because of problems associated with premature birth, she had been advised not to have children. Her pupils became her family. When she noticed that a child was in need of something, she provided it, whether that meant shoes, clothes, visits to the dentist, birthday presents, or old-fashioned caring.

\* \* \* \* \* \* \*

My sister's funeral was scheduled to begin at 1:30 in a church almost sixty miles from the airport. Looking back on that day in November, 1994, and remembering how sad and stressful it was, I

194

have to smile, in spite of myself. It seemed as if some kind of poetic justice was at work making my sister wait after all the times she had made others wait for her. She had often said she would probably be late for her own funeral. I don't think she ever imagined someone else might be late for it as well.

I often wondered how my mother was able to put up with her daughter's chronic lateness, but put up with it she did. I think it helped that mother had the patience of Job and that she had had plenty of opportunity to practice using it before Marie came along. I was almost four years older than my sister. Because I had benefited many times from that store of patience, it did not behoove me to complain about someone else's shortcomings lest my mother go into particulars about the frustration she had had to endure from the likes of me, and how it had nearly driven her to distraction.

I lived my adult life in Minneapolis and St. Paul. The farm, with its rows of walnut trees between my mother's house and my sister's house, was four hours away by car. In the early years I didn't go there very often. Later on that changed.

My Dutch grandfather's farmstead was carefully planned, and in addition to hedges, lawn, flowers, an apple orchard, plum trees, and a grape arbor, he had had a vegetable garden. My father didn't care for gardening. When his parents retired and moved to town, the first thing he did was take out all the strawberry beds.

Years later, after his death, my mother and I decided to restore the vegetable garden. On summer Sunday mornings I sat out there under the Campari umbrella and ate my breakfast. The garden was my refuge, a still, small place surrounded by tall trees, where I could be alone.

I watched my mother drive away to church at 10:30 on Sunday mornings. Worship services started at 11:00. Sometimes I wondered how my sister could be the church organist when she never left for church until shortly before, or even after, 11:00; however, I tried not to think about that. It was none of my business.

One Sunday morning, I decided to go to church with my mother. We left home at 10:30 and entered the sanctuary at 10:45, just in time to hear the pianist begin playing the prelude. At 11:00, the pianist flipped the prelude pages back to the beginning and began playing them all over again. The minister entered the chancel from a side door, sat down in his big chair near the altar, and bowed his head in prayer. Eleven o'clock passed. If the minister prayed for the same thing I was praying for, both prayers went unanswered. When he finished, he opened his eyes and looked around. If he was looking for my sister, he looked in vain. After that he opened his Bible. I wondered if he was, perhaps, checking chapter and verse for the biblical equivalent of Alexander Pope's "Hope springs eternal," or re-reading the Beatitudes to see if there was anything in them about patient people inheriting the earth. After a while, he closed the book and settled back for the duration.

I twisted a little to the right to look at my mother. She was wearing her "I'm in church" face. Then I looked at members of the congregation, thinking some of them, at least, must surely be checking their watches by now, but no one was doing that. The minutes crept by: 11:05, then 11:10, but still no one gave any indication of anything unusual happening. Finally, I realized that, for them, what was happening was not unusual. This was the way it was every Sunday of the year, year in and year out.

Shortly before 11:15, my sister appeared in the narthex. I watched as she walked slowly to the front of the church and sat down in the second row. Compared with my discomfiture, she was a study in composure. Another minute or two passed, but, by now, what did it matter? Then she went to the organ, settled herself comfortably on the bench, and – when she deemed everything good and ready – nodded to the pianist. Together they began playing "Praise God from Whom all Blessings Flow." The congregation stood and sang with gusto.

\* \* \* \* \* \* \*

The Boeing 727 with Sagi on board arrived shortly after 12:30. Sagi had not checked any luggage. She passed her shoulder bag to me, and we rushed out to the car. Traffic was light. We encountered no problems on the way to the small town where the funeral was soon to begin, with or without us. I don't remember that we exceeded the speed limit, but we hurried as the car clock ticked away the minutes.

The funeral bell began tolling as we pulled up in front of the church. There was one parking spot left in the "Reserved for Family" section.

Sagi and I got out of the car and walked up the steps to the church. My Uncle John's son, Stan, saw us coming. He opened the door. My mother was waiting inside, on the landing. Through her tears, she smiled and said, "I knew you'd make it on time." Then she turned and walked up the few steps to the sanctuary. We followed. Together we stood at the open doors for a moment. When the bell stopped ringing, the organ music started. It was 1:30. I looked for my sister and saw her lying in her casket, the pain of her long illness taken from her face by the embalmer's art. She wasn't late for her funeral, and neither were we.

# The Wellstones

Sagi started a two-year postdoctoral fellowship at Duke University in Durham, North Carolina, in 1998. I often visited her there. Once I went by train from Washington, D.C. Other times I flew directly to and from Raleigh-Durham.

One morning Sagi and a friend of hers took me to the airport. As we walked to the departure gate, I noticed someone approaching us with large bags slung over his shoulders, but I didn't pay much attention. I didn't know anyone from North Carolina, and it never occurred to me it might be someone from Minnesota.

We continued on our way. When the shoulder bags came up close, I looked more carefully. It was Paul Wellstone.

"John," he said, "How are you, and what are you doing here in North Carolina?" My first impulse was to say, "Paul," but I wanted to alert Sagi. She had met him at the club, but I wasn't certain she would remember that now, so I said, "Senator Wellstone, what a pleasant surprise, how nice to see you. I'm here visiting my daughter; maybe you remember meeting her at the University Club in St. Paul."

"I do remember," he said, as he held her hand.

I continued, "May I ask what brings you to Raleigh-Durham?"

"Oh," he said, "I went to law school here, and every year they invite me back to give a talk for them."

Sagi joined the conversation, but her friend seemed to have been rendered speechless. It was, I think, the only time in my life when something having to do with me maybe came close to knocking someone's socks off.

\* \* \* \* \* \* \*

I was in France when Senator Paul Wellstone and his wife, Sheila, died in an airplane crash in northern Minnesota. It was Monday, October 25, 2002.

\* \* \* \* \* \* \*

On Sunday mornings when they were in Minnesota, Paul and Sheila Wellstone exercised at the University Club in St. Paul. They lived in the neighborhood and always walked over together. I had a room at the club. Sunday morning was my favorite time for exercising because, until the Wellstones appeared, I usually had the place to myself. They introduced themselves to me the first day. From then on, we always greeted one another. They respected my privacy, and I respected theirs.

The two of them had been coming to the club on a regular basis for several months when one Sunday I noticed that Sheila cut short her routine and was preparing to leave. Paul walked over to where she was standing. It seemed to me as if Sheila had remembered something that needed doing at home. Maybe she had forgotten to turn off the stove, something like that.

After a few minutes, the two of them came over to where I was rowing, and Senator Wellstone said, "Excuse me, John, may we ask a favor?"

I stopped rowing, stood up, and said, "Yes, of course, certainly."

He continued, "Sheila has to go back to the apartment. Would you mind staying on here with me a while longer, until I finish my workout?"

"Not at all," I said. "I'll be happy to do that."

"So, that's taken care of," he said, "good."

They both thanked me. Sheila left, and Paul returned to the Stairmaster. I went back for another round of rowing. When Senator Wellstone finished, he waved goodbye and asked, "See you next week?"

I nodded my head in agreement.

"Good," he said.

Then he was gone.

The next Sunday the two of them were there again. We

greeted one another as usual. A little while later, Sheila told me she was leaving early. Pointing in the direction of her husband, she asked if I would mind staying again. "No problem," I said. "He doesn't like being alone," she added, and left.

From that time on, it was understood that I would stay with him until he was ready to go. I didn't mind. As the weeks passed, it became my job to be there for him. I asked myself if senators are not supposed to be left alone. Years later, I decided it was probably because he already knew he was ill.

I enjoyed the time we spent together, most of it in companionable silence. Sometimes he told me what he had been reading on the airplane on the way out from Washington, D.C., and what it was he would have to read on the way back. It provided me with a glimpse of a world about which I knew very little.

Whenever I saw the Wellstones, they called me by my first name. They asked me to do the same with them. It was easy to say Sheila, and now and then I called him Paul, but if anyone else was present, I always said Senator and Mrs. Wellstone.

They were not Minnesotans by birth, but I think they came to exemplify what is best about the people who live here. I am grateful to have had the chance to make their acquaintance. I know many others who feel the same way. I told myself at the time, long before I was a grandfather, "This will be something to tell my grandchildren," and that's what I am doing now.

In September of 2002, I told the Wellstones I would be

going to France in October to study French for a month, something I had been doing every autumn for several years. They said, "Good luck," and "We'll miss seeing you, but we look forward to hearing all about France and the French when you return. Have a good time. Don't forget us."

Courtesy J. Swenson

University Club, St. Paul

# Fouquet's, Paris

Joann was a volunteer for the Minnesota Opera. She "walked the lights" at rehearsals and always made sure there were plenty of bagels available for cast and crew. Once, she invited me to go to an opera benefit in the walled garden of one of the largest houses on one of the loveliest lakes in the Minneapolis-St. Paul metropolitan area.

By coincidence, I had been acquainted with the previous owner of the house, a pianist. After his death, the house went to his family. Even though none of them could play his Steinway piano, they were proud of its provenance – it had been built in Hamburg – and kept it almost in the middle of the largest room in the house.

As I walked from that room out into the garden, I recognized a neighbor of ours, Bill, a tall, young banker whose father's family owned farms in Iowa. Bill and a lawyer friend of his were engaged in conversation that went beyond being earnest. Both men said, "Hello," and invited me to join them. As I was neighbor to the one and well-enough acquainted with the other, I accepted.

It wasn't long before I caught the gist of their disagreement.

It had to do with French pronunciation. Bill said the legendary restaurant, Fouquet's, located on the Avenue des Champs-Elysées in Paris, rhymed with "who gets." The other man agreed on the first syllable, but insisted that the last syllable rhymed with "Kay's." I was asked for my opinion, but thought it prudent not to give it. If Bill said Fouquet's rhymed with "who gets," one could very well bet one's bottom dollar on that pronunciation. Not only was Bill's mother French, but her maiden name was as well known among the leading families of France as Fouquet's was among knowledgeable people in the restaurant world.

Sagi and I had our own special relationship with Bill's mother. When a friend gave Sagi a French card game called Mille Bornes, Sagi wanted to learn how to pronounce the game's French words and terms. I had not forgotten that Aunt Charlotte used to say, "What little bear doesn't learn, big bear will never master," so I asked Bill if his mother would be willing to help us, and she agreed to do it.

A few days later the telephone rang. Sagi went to answer it. When she returned to the room where I was sitting, she asked, "Do you know someone named Josephine 'Paycare'?"

"No," I said, "I don't, but wasn't there a jazz singer by that name in Paris years ago?"

"Well," said Sagi, "you're going to meet her in a few minutes because she's stopping past to help me with my Mille Bornes pronunciation." It was Bill's mother.

I had always hoped that one day I would have the chance to study French, so I sat in on the pronunciation sessions with Madame "Paycare." Years later, when I began studying French in earnest, I already knew the "r" in French sounds to the American ear much like "w" in English. At the Institute of the Touraine in Tours, located on the Loire River 140 miles southwest of Paris, I didn't have as much trouble pronouncing the name of the town's main avenue, the rue Nationale, as I had with some other words. I pronounced "rue" as if it were spelled "wue" and no one ever questioned it.

Madame "Paycare" taught us well. To make certain we kept the "r" lesson fresh in mind, she reinforced it every time she telephoned by saying, "This is Madame 'Paycare,' as you can probably guess." She always remembered to exaggerate the "r" in the word "probably," so it sounded as if it was spelled "pwobably."

The fact that Bill's mother was French would, by itself, have been sufficient reason to agree with his pronunciation of Fouquet's, but his mother had also shared a little secret with us. Back in the days when women were not allowed to enter Fouquet's unless accompanied by a gentleman, or two, she and Bill's aunts ate lunch there almost every day, even when they were without escorts, because it pleased Fouquet's to make an exception to its rule, just for them.

Champs Elysées

# Johannes Vermeer, 1632–1675

While taking an art history class at the University of Colorado in Boulder, I decided that the Dutch artist Johannes Vermeer was my favorite painter. Through all Sagi's years at home, there was a framed print of *The Milkmaid* on the east wall of her room. We saw *The Lacemaker* at the Louvre in Paris and, a few years later, *Young Woman with a Jug* at the Metropolitan Museum of Art in New York City.

As the years passed, I saw all my favorite Vermeer paintings except one, *The Milkmaid.* It was at the Rijksmuseum in Amsterdam. I sometimes went to Holland, but, whenever I visited there, events seemed to conspire against my seeing that painting. I would arrive at the museum and find it or the gallery closed, or else staff were working on the painting or its frame. For one reason or another, the painting was never on view.

The Dutch consider *The Milkmaid* a national treasure. It rarely leaves the country and was not included in the comprehensive exhibition of Vermeer's work at the National Gallery of Art in Washington, D.C., in the late 1990s. The painting eluded me until one day, returning home from Milan, Italy, I had a layover in the Netherlands.

I took the train into the city, then walked along the canals until I reached the museum. It was open. "Is *The Milkmaid* on display?" I asked. It was. When I reached the gallery, I waited outside for a while before going in. No one else was there. First I looked at the painting from across the room. It didn't seem right to me. Was something wrong with the head? It seemed shrunken and too small for its body. I walked up for a closer look. The first things I noticed were the blue folds in the apron. They were too dark, I thought, almost harsh, and there was so much of that one color. It took me by surprise. I found it ugly. I stepped back, away from the painting, and asked myself why Vermeer had not made this blue more like the refreshing luminous blue he had used in *The Geographer*.

This was as unexpected as it was disconcerting. How was it possible that I had never noticed it before? Copies of this painting had always seemed to radiate calm and quietude. Looking at it early that morning, I found it disturbing.

I thought then, and I wouldn't be surprised to learn now, that it was a fake, perhaps a forgery by the infamous Dutch artist, Han van Meegeren, and not a very good one at that. What was it doing hanging there on the wall in the Rijksmuseum? I checked the lighting to see if a bulb had burned out, and then I thought it might be a joke. I turned around and looked out in the hall to see if people there were laughing at my consternated state. "Maybe

I'm on *Candid Camera*," I thought, "and that is why no one else is here." I imagined a child walking in and saying, "The milkmaid is not wearing a single brush stroke of anything painted by Vermeer," but no child appeared. Maybe the precious original had been locked up and hidden away in a vault somewhere, like some of the famous statues and sculptures in Italy. I took out my glasses and examined it again.

I wondered what Sagi thought about this painting. Through all her growing-up years, a large print of *The Milkmaid* had been in her room; it was there when she went to sleep at night and when she woke up in the morning. We had never really talked about it. It was like the air we breathed. Had she taken the picture for granted, like the furniture, or had she seen serenity in it, as I did?

Everyone knows that a copy can be misleading and quite different from the original, but these differences were startling. I decided to ask Sagi about it, but by the time I arrived home, I had changed my mind.

I went to Sagi's room. She was working at her desk and waved me in. I sat down facing the painting. There she was, the milkmaid, standing quietly at her work table. When Sagi looked over at me, I asked, "How would you define the word calm?"

"Calm," she said, and repeated the question. "What is calm? For me, it is all a matter of appearances. I would say it's like the swan who seems serene to all who gaze upon her, but we must not forget that while the swan appears to glide effortlessly along, she is, in fact, paddling furiously down below. And remember, if we want to be regarded as calm, it helps to get up early in the morning."

"Is that all there is to it?" I wondered, but I said nothing. No mention of the milkmaid, even though she was right there in front of us. It may have had no effect on Sagi whatsoever. If that was the case, I didn't want to know, so I never asked, and she never said.

\* \* \* \* \* \* \*

Years later, while reading a book my friend Herb had given me – Martin Bailey's *Vermeer* (Phaidon, London, 1995) – I saw these words: ". . . and at first glance Vermeer's pictures convey great tranquility, although the viewer soon senses the tensions that lurk beneath the surface." Yes, I realized, that's right. *The Milkmaid*, like the swan, was a juxtaposition of tranquility and tension. Now I knew. I didn't have to ask. Sagi had understood.

# Vegetable Garden

The French word for a vegetable garden is *potager*. Guidebooks say the finest *potager* in France is at the Château de Villandry, about ten miles west of Tours, in the Touraine. Many travel brochures for Villandry show the château in the background, with purple cabbages arranged in geometric patterns in the foreground.

After taking retirement, I decided to study French in Tours. I made a dozen trips in as many years, usually in October, when the purple cabbages at Villandry were at their best. After seeing Villandry the first time, I decided to add purple cabbages to the vegetable garden at the farm.

Vegetables have some advantages over flowers: they are easier to grow, easier to weed, and they can be eaten. Vegetables are usually planted in rows because that facilitates harvesting. When the season is over, the garden is quickly cleared, and one can begin dreaming about next year's crop.

Friends sometimes asked me why I wanted a vegetable garden. It was hard to explain how important my grandfather's town garden had been to me when I was growing up, so I just told them I wanted to grow purple cabbages. When they saw the photos, it was easier for them to understand my enthusiasm.

There was a clearing in the grove of cottonwood trees near our farmhouse. That space and the trees around it reminded me of the illustrations for Mr. McGregor's garden in Beatrix Potter's *Peter Rabbit* books.

My garden also had rabbits. I had to build something to keep them out. Digging post holes for a wire fence was more work than I could manage. Hedges take a long time to grow, and rabbits can always find a way through them. Any kind of wall would have been too expensive. Back in the 1950s, I had built split-rail fences for horseback jumping in the west pasture, but now I needed something sturdier. I remembered seeing old railroad ties lying along a stretch of abandoned railroad track a few miles away. The owner was glad to be rid of them. By midwinter, thanks to our neighbors, the Slaters, and their big red truck, I had the two hundred ties I needed to enclose an area that measured forty by sixty feet.

As I built the wooden fence, I wove wire mesh between the ties so rabbits couldn't get in. The following spring I staked out four square vegetable beds inside the fenced area. I left room between the beds for paths that I planned to add at a later date.

The spaces between the vegetable beds and the fence were devoted mostly to crocuses, tulips, peonies, irises, delphinium, monkshood, and Minnesota wildflowers.

As the years passed, I gathered old sidewalk pavers and built paths around the four squares. That made it easy to enjoy the garden on rainy days. On sunny days I sat out there on the shady side and relished the solitude. In some ways it reminded me of contemplative gardens in Japan. I remember being told, years ago, that in order to clear one's mind, one should try to imagine a pond in the middle of a

Farm Garden, Minnesota

forest. I tried doing this, but it wasn't long before I noticed that my imagination had replaced the pond with my garden. The substitution has stayed with me, and today, when I find myself trying to tame a multitude of tumultuous thoughts, I sit down and try to remember the quiet at the farm.

It was a tranquil place, an inward-looking garden. The neat rows of vegetables were easy to cultivate. Plants that could obscure

*215*

the architecture of the garden were relegated to adjunct locations beyond the garden fence, where it didn't matter if they grew large or spread themselves out.

I planted purple cabbages wherever there was room. They are hardy in our garden zone, and in the years when the frost came late, they kept their wonderful purple color until mid-December.

My garden wasn't as good as my Dutch grandfather's hedged garden had been, but it was good enough for me. I was happy to have been able enough to build it.

*  *  *  *  *  *  *

It was early evening when Sagi and her husband saw the garden for the first time. We watched the sun go down behind the Blue Mounds, eighteen miles to the west. I closed my eyes. Looking back more than half a century, I saw again the big cottonwood trees flanking the lane that led from the garden out to the wetland. I could see the boy who never tired of listening to the rustle of starchy leaves in the cottonwood canopy high above him. I remembered what my grandmother had told me about life on the prairie in the late 1800s, when she was young. Native Americans had sometimes stopped at the farm and talked about the "Great Encroachment."

On the west slope of Buffalo Ridge in the southwesternmost county of Minnesota, more than a thousand acres of what is now Blue Mounds State Park were once part of the vast mid-continent hunting grounds of the Plains and Prairie people. The Blue Mounds, together with Pipestone Quarry twenty-five miles to the north (where peace pipes were fashioned), constitute an ancient and revered part of history. The mounds are known for the blue haze that often enshrouds them and for the buffalo that still roam there. Rock climbers use the cliff formations now, but Buffalo Leap is not forgotten.

Buffalo

# Labyrinth

Sagi and I had forgotten the road map in Paris, yet by some small miracle, we found our way to Chartres. Driving through the grain fields we'd read about and seen in pictures, we saw the cathedral in the distance. It was much larger than we had imagined and seemed to expand and rise as we approached until its parapets and buttresses loomed above us. Something of the awe that pilgrims to this place have talked about for centuries seemed to come down and settle on us.

We found a parking space just in time to join a group led by an Englishman who first visited Chartres when he was a young man. He had been so moved by the experience that he decided to spend the rest of his life there. The tour began with the windows above the front entrance. They were familiar to us because at home we had a large picture puzzle made in Italy that rendered the colors of the glass in these windows about as faithfully as technology permits. For us, this was the most beautiful glass in all of France. After looking at the windows, we walked the labyrinth before going on to the transept.

Our preferred rose window in France is the one on the south

side of Notre Dame Cathedral in Paris. We could see it from our favorite restaurant. At Chartres Cathedral, the rose window on the left as one approaches the altar reminded us of children's richly colored building blocks caught tumbling about in a black circle. The blue colors were lovely, ethereal.

It has been said that the blue glass made at Chartres in the twelfth century is as different from the blue glass made there in the twentieth century as night is from day. I don't know about that, but the blue glass made at Chartres after World War II and used in the sanctuary windows at the Kaiser Wilhelm Gedächtniskirche in Berlin, for example, seems to be missing a crucial ingredient. Perhaps it is something found in nature. Not many people at Chartres knew exactly how the glass was made. As the centuries passed, the process was forgotten, or lost. Since that time, those who work with stained glass have not been able to learn the secret of Chartres glass made in the Middle Ages, nor have they been able to match it in a chemistry lab. This deficiency, what the French call *le manque*, makes the glass in Germany's capital city less compelling.

We left the cathedral by a side door. In a small shop in the town we bought a drawing of the labyrinth. A year or two later we had it framed. One winter we made a maze pattern in the snow on a university soccer field. Another time we made one on our lawn and used it for playing Fox and Goose.

In the late 1990s, a canvas copy of the labyrinth at Chartres was exhibited at Duke University. Sagi sent me a large poster of it.

From this I made a pattern and staked it out in the tallgrass prairie that lies between my garden at the farm and the creek that runs past the old orchard. When I completed all the measuring, I got on the riding mower and made my own labyrinth. The cattle on the other side of the half-mile line fence heard the small tractor, looked up, and then went back to their grazing.

As I worked on the labyrinth, I thought about the twists and turns our lives take as we pass through our years here on earth. When I finished the job, I noticed that the cattle had moved farther down the valley. The Minotaur from Greek mythology came to mind, and I wondered if there was something about my labyrinth that the Black Angus bull over in the pasture didn't like.

Labyrinth

# Cavatina

"Herb," I said, "there is a problem with the music. We have had several meetings with the next of kin, but we are no closer to a solution now than when we first began. There is another meeting scheduled for tomorrow afternoon at five o'clock. I'm calling to ask if you can sit in on it. Adding you to the mix might be just what's needed to get this resolved. I'll take you to lunch or dinner, maybe both. Just call me. I'm carrying my cell phone. *Ciao!*" I turned the ringer off, crossed my fingers for a moment, and then accelerated down the ramp into the fray of freeway traffic. Driving would take my mind off the music.

Herb's reply was on the phone when I arrived at the mausoleum an hour later: "Received your message. I'll see you tomorrow at five. Dinner would work for us. Tell me what's been suggested in the way of music. Give me the reasons why each was rejected. We are at the Bakken tonight. Leave a message. *Skål!*"

One by one, I went over the objections that had been made. The organ in the chapel was so bad no one wanted to play it. The older brother said the piano was tinny and sounded like something played at a poor man's wedding. The younger brother felt that pairing a violin with the piano would only work if the service were held in a barn. His wife opposed having a singer because, in her words, "It feeds into the whole 'cult of personality' thing." However, everyone agreed that the music was the most important part of the memorial program.

I called and left the message. Early the next morning there was an answer waiting: "Hire a string quartet to play the cavatina from Beethoven's thirteenth quartet."

"Easy for you to say, Horatio," I thought, but I called the family, and they all approved of the idea. The five o'clock meeting was cancelled.

Now all I had to do was find a string quartet. The main problem was always that one or two players hadn't performed the piece for a while. Just a few days would not give them enough time to rehearse. Finally, Vali Phillips called to say he had good news and bad news: four members of the Minnesota Orchestra, including himself, knew the music, but they refused to play because they no longer accepted requests for weddings, funerals, and parties. It took up too much time.

The chapel director overheard the conversation and said, "If it's time they are concerned about, I have a solution for you." He showed me a room separated from the chapel by a heavy curtain. This room had a private entrance.

"The quartet can use this room," he said. "The service begins at one o'clock, but the quartet doesn't play until after two, right? They can come in fifteen minutes early, and when it's time for them to play, we will open the curtain. They can perform the cavatina. When they're finished, we'll close the curtain, and they're out of here. An hour, max. Call him back."

I called back. Mr. Phillips and the other members of the Minneapolis Quartet liked the idea, and that's the way it happened. Everyone was pleased with how well it worked. Beethoven's music was beautiful. While the quartet was playing, I think we all, in our various ways, said good-bye to the man lying in the cherry wood casket at the front of the room. I had worried that the curtain might malfunction, but it didn't. Sophie, my granddaughter, paid rapt attention as it slowly opened and, twenty minutes later, closed, just as smooth as silk.

The service continued, and we went on to remember the life of our beloved brother and friend.

String Quartet

# Gettysburg

I.      Cemetery Ridge

I am grateful to Anne B. Hage for collecting information about what happened at Cemetery Ridge, to Leona Carlson and Joyce Cobb at the Hennepin County Library in Minneapolis for finding it, and to Anne Kaplan, Editor of *Minnesota History*, for helping me use it.

On July 2, 1863, the First Minnesota Regiment found itself at Gettysburg. It was the most crucial time of the Civil War. The Union line was in danger of breaking apart. Victory seemed imminent for the Confederate South. Reinforcements were on the way, but General Winfield Scott Hancock needed to hold the line together until they could arrive. The Confederates were closing in. It was a matter of yards and minutes.

When an opening appeared in the line along the ridge, General Hancock called for help in filling it. A few more than 250 men appeared. Hancock asked, "What regiment is this?"

"The First Minnesota," he was told.

"Is that all we have?" Hancock wanted to know. When the answer came in the affirmative, he called them into battle. To gain a few minutes time, he was asking them for sacrifice, and they knew it.

Colonel William Colvill gave the order to go forward at double-quick march, bayonets at the ready, directly into the center of the Confederate line. Even though the Minnesota regiment was vastly outnumbered, it deployed quickly and charged into the deadly fire of the enemy.

The boldness of the charge and the speed with which it was carried out surprised and confounded the Southerners. They saw enemy infantry heading toward their front at the double-quick, bayonets bared. The Rebels abandoned their forward posts and fell back to the second line. The Minnesotans kept going and were met by a devastating hail of rifle fire.

In the next few minutes, Confederate blasts from more than a thousand rifles, backed by artillery, swept along the length of the hundred-yard line, lacerating the Minnesota soldiers. The men of the First Minnesota took cover in a dry stream bed bordered by brush, firing all the while, giving it everything they had.

When it was over, almost all the Minnesota commanding field officers had been killed. By conservative estimates, two of every three Minnesotans were dead, while half of those left alive were wounded, including Colonel Colvill. One witness counted more than a dozen men dead in an area roughly the size of a school classroom.

This battle constituted the carnage and horror of war at its most salient, but the line held. The battle was over. The South had been repulsed. The First Minnesota had given Hancock the precious few minutes he needed, plus some to spare, and it had been enough. The reinforcements had arrived. The main Union line had not been breached.

G. W. Hosmer, writing in *The New York Herald*, told how those still alive did what they could to help the wounded, and then, when they were finished, lay down on the ground, exhausted, and slept side by side with the dead.

As President Abraham Lincoln foresaw, the world has not forgotten what happened at Gettysburg. We still honor those from both sides who perished there.

First Minnesota Regiment monument, Gettysburg

II.      Governor Jesse Ventura

One hundred fourteen years after the Civil War ended, Sagi went with her sixth-grade class to visit the Gettysburg battlefield and its monuments of remembrance. Like so many Americans and others from around the world before and since, she has not forgotten that experience. Friends, relatives, and school personnel gathered at the airport to wait for the sixth-graders to return. Across the runway to the south, we could see Fort Snelling National Cemetery where many veterans of the Civil War, including some from the First Minnesota Regiment, are buried. From the north side of the terminal building one can see historic Fort Snelling, which overlooks the Mississippi River. Sagi's school was three miles upriver from the fort's round tower.

Everyone watched as the DC-10 pulled up to the gate. A little while later the youngsters appeared. When Sagi came up to us, I asked, "How was the trip?"

"So many soldiers died there," she said.

* * * * * * *

Twenty years later, on January 4, 1999, Jesse Ventura was inaugurated Governor of Minnesota. During the preceding gubernatorial campaign in 1998, Sagi had called from Charleston, South Carolina, to ask which candidate I was supporting. I hadn't given much attention to the campaign other than to note that neither the Democratic nor the

Republican candidate had generated much enthusiasm among the electorate.

"I will probably vote for Attorney General 'Skip' Humphrey," I said. "You know his father once wrote me a letter."

"I remember," Sagi said, "and you still have it, but what about Jesse Ventura, who's running as an Independent. He seems to be causing some excitement, at least out here in the Carolinas, land of scuppernong."

I had no idea who Jesse Ventura was, but he was elected, served one term, and then, after the usual slings and arrows that assail politicians, retired, leaving the state with the welcome memory of a colorful personality who will liven up junior high school history classes for a long time to come.

During Governor Ventura's term, the Minnesota Historical Society received a letter from the State of Virginia. The First Minnesota Regiment had captured a banner of the 28th Virginia Regiment at Gettysburg. A Virginia historical re-enactment group was asking for its return. There was a lot of restrained jostling back and forth on the subject before Governor Ventura, a former professional wrestler, stepped in. Recalling the grievous loss of life suffered by the First Minnesota at Gettysburg and pointing out that a flag is not the same as a prisoner of war, Mr. Ventura quietly settled the matter by saying, "If Virginia wants the flag, let them come and get it."

# Soup Bowls with Handles

We went to Berlin to visit Charlottenburg Castle in 1981. In the park behind the castle there was a small building several stories high that housed a porcelain collection. It was not as grand as the porcelain museum in Dresden, but Sagi and I enjoyed the exhibits. When we came to soup bowls with handles, we had our usual conversation about them.

There were soup bowls with handles at home, and we enjoyed sipping soup from them, but we stopped doing that in front of other people after someone told us that sipping soup from bowls made us look like two little pigs visiting the trough for the first time.

\* \* \* \* \* \* \*

Last year I was invited to celebrate Thanksgiving with friends in Palm Springs. One of the house guests was Makoto, a man whose father had been the official translator for the Japanese Embassy in Rome, but the reason I've not forgotten him is that he and his family had once met the Pope. During that visit, Makoto's father, mother, and sisters were invited to kiss the Pope's ring. They did so, but to the dismay of everyone concerned, when it came time for Makoto, who was the youngest, to do the same, he refused. No amount of cajoling could make him change his mind. After what seemed like a foretaste of eternity, the family retired from the Pontiff's presence, leaving the Pope's ring unkissed by Makoto.

One day, while visiting a consignment shop, Makoto and I were looking at soup bowls with handles. They were made by Limoges. I figured that if anyone of my acquaintance could answer the question about sipping soup from bowls with handles, it might very well be someone who had refused to kiss the Pope's ring. Sure enough, Makoto knew the answer. "If it's a thin soup," he said, "with no lumps or other things in it, it is not incorrect to take the bowl by the handles and sip from it."

I wish I had known this when Sagi was a child, but I didn't.

# Frank Lloyd Wright, 1869-1959

I.      Neighborhood Influence

When I lived in Chicago in the 1960s, I walked past Frank Lloyd Wright's Robie house almost every day. Sagi saw it for the first time in the 1970s.

We never saw "Northome," the house that Mr. Wright built west of Minneapolis for the Francis Little family. It was taken down in the early 1970s, but thanks to Thomas Hoving at the Metropolitan Museum of Art in New York City, its living room was saved and re-assembled in the Metropolitan's American Wing.

Our favorite Wright house was in Prospect Park in Minneapolis. We knew its owner. It was a few minutes away by car from where we lived in St. Anthony Park in St. Paul. The Wright house is still there. It sits high on a hill that overlooks the length of the Mississippi River Gorge between Minneapolis and St. Paul.

Three lawns and a street separated us from a house that was modeled after one that Wright built into a hillside in Madison, Wisconsin. On Hoyt Avenue, across the street from the architect-designed houses in

University Grove (some of which remind people of Wright's work), the house epitomizes the kind of well-reasoned space that provides a place for everything, thus making neatness a daily pleasure.

Down the street and around the corner of our block, an architect lived with his family in what we called the "Big Sur" house. It, too, sat on a hillside.

The Prospect Park house, the Hoyt house, and the "Big Sur" house would not be out of place in Sarah Susanka's book *The Not So Big House*. Not too big, not too small, they were, in our opinion, just right.

Like many of Wright's admirers, we wondered what inspired his Prairie House. He was often asked, but never answered this question. If the idea for the Prairie House had been original with him, I think he would have taken credit for it. It may be he did not answer the question because he did not want people to know – it would have been bad for his image – that he used sources that were not his own, especially for the Prairie House, of which he was so justly proud and which did so much to make his reputation.

So what are the origins of those long, low, hipped-roof houses with the grand overhangs and great rooms? Who first constructed buildings that were essentially one room wide, like "Northome" on Lake Minnetonka?

After more than fifty years of paying attention to architecture, especially in the United States, France, and Japan, my answer to that question can be found in the next story.

## II.    The Prairie House

The roof of an Alpine chalet lends itself well to a snowy environment. Thatched roofs are found in rainy parts of the world. The Japanese use lightweight materials for their traditional roofs so people will not be crushed during earthquakes. Cottages along the Dutch and German coasts of the North Sea are built with hipped roofs because this shape roof – four sloping sides, no gables – is less likely to be damaged by the strong winds that characterize that region.

Early settlers on the American plains and prairies dug storm cellars for shelter from the violent windstorms that are not unusual in that part of the country.

As railroads expanded throughout the Midwest, more people learned of the wind's power. Well before 1900, it was common knowledge that blizzard winds of winter were sometimes strong enough to move a locomotive off railroad tracks. (One hundred years later, one of the world's largest wind turbine colonies is being constructed on Minnesota's Buffalo Ridge.) During a snowstorm in February, 2001, the wind blew an 18-wheeler truck off Interstate 90 in South Dakota. News of this event was carried on national television, but most Midwesterners know all about the wind's awesome power. They are not surprised by what it can do.

Railway companies took care to protect their property. They hired the best architects they could find, people like Edward Burling (1819-1892) and Henry Van Brunt (1832-1903). In the days before Frank

Lloyd Wright, many young American architects studied in France. For example, Henry Hobson Richardson (1838-1886) studied at the École des Beaux Arts in Paris in the early 1860s. He apprenticed with a French architect who specialized in railway depot design. When these young architects returned to the United States, they often adapted French design to meet American conditions. In the Midwest, they lowered the pitch of the roof, making it flatter and less likely to be caught by the wind.

The hipped roof, with its sloping sides, is about as close as a roof can get to the shape of the earthen mound that covers a storm cellar. It does a good job of meeting the demands that wind and weather place on buildings in open country.

The railroads could not afford ramshackle buildings (of which there were many on the frontier) that could easily be bent out of shape during windstorms. Many railroad depot buildings cost a considerable amount of money, but they more than paid for themselves in the long run.

Depots with hipped roofs became a familiar sight on the prairie. In 1898 the Omaha Company completed its new passenger depot in Worthington, Minnesota, about fifty miles from the point where Iowa, Minnesota, and South Dakota meet. The price tag was $10,000, a lot of money in those days.

Today that depot building – its waiting room windows following a pattern one sometimes sees in apartments on the Boulevard Haussmann in Paris – is in need of some repairs, but is still in relatively good condition. Like the more handsome depot in Luverne, Minnesota, thirty miles to the west, it is a good example of the railroad depot architecture that one finds throughout the Midwest.

From the beginning, these depots were admired by the people in the communities they served. Long and low, they looked right at home on the prairie, as if they had been waiting patiently for the railroad to arrive. Their quiet, unbroken lines combined with generous planes and proportions to enhance and complement the beauty of the gently rolling hills of the prairie. With broad roofs and overhangs, plus spacious porches and platforms that extended the horizontal line of the building out along the railroad tracks and into the distance, the depots seemed to be a kind of summary statement of the prairie itself.

Like the railroad tracks, these buildings seemed bolted to the ground. No one doubted the integrity of their foundations. They gave the impression that it would take a lot more than a high wind out of the southwest to dislodge them. These were sturdy buildings, practical and unpretentious; they were a good match for the people who settled here, and, like them, the depots had come to stay.

More than a hundred years have passed since the first hipped-roof depots appeared in the American heartland. For the last fifty of those years, most people in the United States have traveled most of the time by car and airplane. Many of them regard railroad depots as a thing of the past, but these buildings still have a powerful hold on the American imagination and are not forgotten. In dozens of small towns and cities, people have worked hard to make sure the depots will be there for generations to come. One finds railway depots all across the plains and prairies. Some of them have been moved to parks; others serve as museums, and a few are still doing the work for which they were intended. Whatever their role, they serve as tangible reminders of the way things used to be, of what the West was like.

Taken as a group, the railroad depots of the Midwest are among the most interesting buildings in America. Long before Frank Lloyd Wright spoke of "organic" architecture, the architects of these depots presented us with a remarkable partnering of land and building.

In my opinion, Mr. Wright found the inspiration for his Prairie House in these long, low, hipped-roof railroad depots. There was one in Richland Center, Wisconsin, the town where he was born. Others like it dotted the landscape of Wisconsin and Illinois. Mr. Wright saw them every time he took the train to Chicago and back.

# Flag Day

The house to the north of ours was on a corner. It blocked our view of the property across the street from it, so we could never see the people who lived there, not even when they left their house or returned to it. We never saw them take in their mail, mow their lawn, or shovel the sidewalk. We would not have recognized them if they had bumped into us.

For years we lived a stone's throw away, yet when they died, I did not know their name; even so, I was always aware that they were there. Something about that house stood out. It was kept up about as well as most of the houses in this part of St. Anthony Park, but there was something forlorn about it. I don't recall any of our neighbors, all of whom had lived near that corner longer than we had, ever mentioning that family.

And then one day a friend of ours from out of town told us that only an old man and his wife lived there. Our friend knew this because she was related to them, but hadn't seen them for years. We were surprised. That's all she said. We did not ask any questions.

The St. Anthony Park Association met once a month in the Episcopal church basement. I was not a member, but someone once invited me to a meeting. The after-dinner speaker was Robert Anderson, pastor at the local Lutheran church. From what I heard later, I wasn't the only one who was surprised by the stern tone of his remarks. Many of those present had expected a pat on the back in recognition of all the good works the association did in the community.

Mr. Anderson talked instead about the people who lived in St. Anthony Park and the four P's: patriotic, Protestant, proud, and provincial. The first two words were acceptable enough to those who heard him speak that evening, but the last two stung a little. Members of Pastor Anderson's congregation regarded him as clever, an intellectual even. He must have known he was placing his listeners in something of a bind, for if some among the well-traveled audience had dared to complain about being called provincial, it would only have been regarded by others as proof of their being proud. Not long after that speech, the pastor and his family moved away.

The next time I saw homeowners hanging out their flags, I remembered what the minister had said. I began paying more attention to which houses flew the flag and which ones did not.

One Flag Day I noticed that every house in sight was flying the flag. The house at the top of our street had a flag draped across its living room windows. Later that same day, Sagi and I went for a walk. The forlorn house was not displaying a flag. We wondered why not, and then I remembered.

The year we bought our house I had been working in the alley on the Fourth of July when I heard children's voices. From the alley I could see the house across from the corner house. There was a three-foot-high stone wall along the sidewalk in front of it. I saw several children marching down the sidewalk. They were carrying small American flags stapled to sticks. Every few feet the children stopped, leaned over the wall, stuck a flag in the ground, and then continued on their way. I thought it looked nice.

I went back to work. A minute or two later, I heard a screen door slam. An elderly gentleman, whom I took to be the neighbor whose lawn was now festooned with flags, came out on the porch; he walked down the steps and along the retaining wall. One after the other, he pulled the flags out of the ground and broke the sticks in half. Then he crumpled the flags and put them in his jacket pocket. When he finished, he went back in the house.

* * * * * * *

In 2008, I learned that the man and his wife had had two sons. Both young men served during World War II. The older was a Second Lieutenant with the Army-Air Force 802nd Bomb Squadron; he died July 7, 1944, and was buried at Fort Snelling National Cemetery in

June of 1949. His brother was a Private First Class with the 517th Parachute Infantry 13th Airborne Division; he was buried at Fort Snelling fifteen months later.

# Holland Park

I was tired, but it had been a while since I'd watched a British comedy, so I checked the public television channel before turning out the lights. I recognized one of the actors, Geoffrey Palmer. He had played the dentist in *Butterflies*. I liked him, so I sat down on the sofa to watch the program and soon fell asleep, but I remember someone mentioning Holland Park, in London. I knew where that was. We had stayed there in 1976. Barker's, the less well-known London department store, was close by and so was the International Children's Book Centre, where we were members. Kenneth Grahame, the Scottish writer, had lived in that part of the city for a time.

To prepare for the London visit, we played a board game called London Cabbie and worked on a puzzle that depicted the London Underground.

On the evening of our arrival, we had – like Christopher Robin and Alice – gone down to Buckingham Palace. There was a crowd. We watched as the Queen passed slowly by, an arm's length away, in one of her older Rolls-Royce cars. Her dinner guest, Valéry Giscard d'Estaing, the President of France, was riding with her. They were on their way to the opera. We walked all the way back to our hotel, through streets filled with people so diverse and vibrant it was like being part of an international bazaar. Samuel Johnson got it right when he said, "He who is tired of London is tired of life."

Back at the hotel, as we sat on the balcony of our apartment drinking grapefruit juice, a Concorde flew low over the city, heading for Heathrow. Its turned-down nose reminded us of an anteater.

It was the hottest summer England had experienced in 200 years. I remember it well, as if it had all taken place yesterday. We shopped at Barker's. We bought a few books at Foyles and spent a lot of time reading at the International Children's Book Centre. We ordered books from its reading guides two or three times a year. When the "London books" arrived in the mail, we celebrated.

We walked along Rotten Row. "Look," said Sagi, "it's like Summit Avenue in St. Paul, but instead of joggers between the rows of trees, there are people on horseback." At home Sagi went horseback riding occasionally, but she was not yet ten years old, and we thought she was too young to try it here. Instead, we walked along the Serpentine, visited Madame Tussaud's, and saw Paddington Station. We went to the zoo, passed the British Museum, and ended up at Piccadilly Circus. At Fortnum & Mason we found ourselves in the middle of a fashion show and were surprised by all the canned goods on the shelves of that fabled emporium. We bought an umbrella touting the British flag at John Smith's, where they addressed me as "Governor."

From there we went to St. Martin-in-the-Fields. I stumbled and fell as I stepped up to take a seat in one of the pews. I was able to go on to Westminster Abbey, but sat down at the first opportunity, in too much pain to visit the Poets' Corner. At Victoria Station, we wondered if anyone had ever really left a baby in a handbag there, the way Miss Prism says it happened in Oscar Wilde's *The Importance of Being Earnest.*

We rode in taxis, on double-decker buses (always on top), and took the Underground from High Street Kensington Station. We saw Royal Albert Hall, St. Paul's Cathedral, the Tower of London, and the Tower Bridge nearby. We went to Harrods, but not at tea time, and walked through the Burlington Arcade. We saw the British Design Centre from which we had, a year or two earlier, ordered two no-nonsense nutcrackers that later came to remind us of medieval instruments of torture.

How had we managed to do it all? And where has the time gone since then? Sagi grew up, went away to school, found a job, married, and has a family now.

\* \* \* \* \* \* \*

I woke up later that night, turned off the television, and went to bed. The next evening I watched another episode in the series featuring Holland Park. In addition to Geoffrey Palmer, it stars Dame Judi Dench. She and I are almost the same age. I watch as the two of them leave their house. I think I recognize it. They walk out into Holland Park where Sagi and I walked more than thirty years ago.

I like the name of the program, *As Time Goes By*. It is apt and resonates with me, as I am sure it does with many others of a certain age. I think about time and remember my grandmother looking at her wedding picture. "We were so young," she said. There was such longing and sadness in her voice that I thought her heart would break right there in front of me. I could feel how much she would have liked returning to the time when the photo was taken, if only for an instant, but she couldn't. No one can.

Now I am a grandfather. Although I try to resist, it is my turn to be old, to look back and try to remember, for my granddaughter's sake. Yes, my own sweet child, time goes by. There is no way to stop it. That's the thing about time — it passes.

Garden Gate

# Afterword

Writing down on paper a few of life's happenings can be a rich experience. It has helped me hold close some of the people, places, and things that have played important parts in an odyssey that now comprises more than seven decades.

It is never too late to share with others what we remember. No matter which one of the several arts we choose to employ in this endeavor, it will enhance our understanding of the role we have in life's grand pageant.

John Elsing
Minneapolis
2012

Street Sweeper, Paris

# In Memoriam

John Elsing

Mother

Mary Elsing
1911-2011

Made in the USA
San Bernardino, CA
04 April 2015